FERAL ANIMALS

Books LLC®, Wiki Series, Memphis, USA, 2011. ISBN: 9781157167587. www.booksllc.net
Copyright: http://creativecommons.org/licenses/by-sa/3.0/deed.en

Table of Contents

Alexandrine Parakeet	1
American Mink	4
Arapawa Island (sheep)	11
Australian feral camel	11
Burmese Pythons in Florida	14
Campbell Island sheep	15
Canadian Parliamentary Cats	16
Donkey	16
Eastern Rosella	21
Feral	22
Feral Pigeon	25
Feral cat	28
Feral chicken	31
Feral horse	31
Feral parrots	33
Ferret	35
Free-ranging urban dog	38
Help Joey	39
Indian pariah dog	40
Monk Parakeet	41
Ossabaw Island Hog	44
Overpopulation in companion animals	45
Pariah dog	45
Rabbits in Australia	46
Rainbow Lorikeet	48
Red-crowned Amazon	50
Red-eared slider	50
Red-masked Parakeet	54
Rose-ringed Parakeet	55
Santa Cruz sheep	57
Sato (dog)	57
Semi-feral	58
Stray dogs in Bangkok	58
Sulphur-crested Cockatoo	58
Trap-Neuter-Return	60
Wild boar	61
Yellow-crested Cockatoo	68

Introduction

Purchase of this book entitles you to a free trial membership in the publisher's book club at www.booksllc.net. (Time limited offer.) Simply enter the barcode number from the back cover onto the membership form. The book club entitles you to select from hundreds of thousands of books at no additional charge. You can also download a digital copy of this and related books to read on the go. Simply enter the title or subject onto the search form to find them.

Each chapter in this book ends with a URL to a hyperlinked online version. Type the URL exactly as it appears. If you change the URL's capitalization it won't work. Use the online version to access related pages, websites, footnotes, tables, color photos, updates. Click the version history tab to see the chapter's contributors. Click the edit link to suggest changes.

A large and diverse editor base collaboratively wrote the book, not a single author. After a long process of discussion and debate, the chapters gradually took on a neutral point of view reached through consensus. Additional editors expanded and contributed to chapters striving to achieve balance and comprehensive coverage. This reduced the regional or cultural bias found in many other books and provided access and breadth on subject matter otherwise little documented.

Alexandrine Parakeet

The **Alexandrine Parakeet** or **Alexandrian Parrot** (*Psittacula eupatria*) is a member of the psittaciformes order and of the psittacines family. The species is named after Alexander the Great, who is credited with the exporting of numerous specimens of this bird from Punjab into various European and Mediterranean countries and regions, where they were considered prized possessions for the nobles and royalty.

The species name *eupatria* has its origins from Latin and/or could be a Greco-Latin combination. Where the prefix *eu* translates into *good or noble* and the suffix *patria* is a Latin word translating into *fatherland or ancestry*. Consequently, the scientific name means *of noble fatherland or of noble ancestry*.

Sub-species with distribution

The following sub-species, many of them allopatric are recognised based on geographical distribution:

- *Psittacula eupatria eupatria*, Alexandrine Parakeet (nominate race) - East India to Hyderabad, Andhra Pradesh in the South, Sri Lanka.
- *Psittacula eupatria avensis*, Indo-Burmese Alexandrine Parakeet - Northeast India to Amherst in Myanmar
- *Psittacula eupatria magnirostris*, Andaman Islands' Alexandrine Parakeet - Andaman Islands
- *Psittacula eupatria nipalensis*, Nepalese Alexandrine Parakeet - Eastern Afghanistan, Pakistan, North and central India, Nepal, Bhutan to Assam in Northeast India.

- *Psittacula eupatria siamensis*, Laos' or Siamese Alexandrine Parakeet - Vietnam, Cambodia, Laos, north and east Thailand

The species has naturalized (species that live and reproduce outside its natural distribution range) itself in numerous European countries. Particularly in Germany, in the south of England, in Belgium, in western Turkey and in the Netherlands where it generally lives amongst or along side flocks of naturalized *Psittacula krameri* (Ringnecked or Rose-ringed Parakeet).

The Alexandrine Parakeet's call is a powerful screech but deeper than that of its very close-relative the *Psittacula krameri* (Ringnecked or Rose-Ringed Parakeet)

Description

Male

Female

The Alexandrine Parakeet is a large Parakeet species measuring 58 cm (23 in) in total length with a wingspan averaging 18.9–21.5 cm (7.5–8.5 in). It is mainly green with a blue-grey sheen on its cheeks and napes, particularly in males. The abdomen is yellowish-green, the upperside of the middle tail feathers is blueish-green, the upperside of the external tail feathers is green while the underside of the tail feathers are all yellow. All Alexandrine Parakeets (irrespective of age, gender and/or sub-species) boldly display a maroon (reddish-brown) patch at the top of their wing coverts (commonly called 'shoulder' patch). The shoulder patch is seen in parakeets at their first feathering before fledging from their nests. The lower and upper mandible are red with yellow tips. The adult's irises are yellowish-white and the periopthalmic rings are light grey. The legs are grey except in the *P. e. siamensis* (Laos' or Siamese sub-species) where they are yellowish-grey.

The species is dimorphic in adulthood (3 years and older). The immatures are monomorphic and are similar but duller in appearance to that of the adult females. Adult males always show pitch-black neck rings and large pink bands on their napes (commonly called nape bands). Often males only display a little band of blueish-grey above their bold pink nape-bands. Adult females frequently show neck ring shadows that are anywhere between light and dark shades of grey. Females never display true black feathers in their neck-rings. Immatures of either genders are very similar to adult females but as with all genuine parakeet species, the young Alexandrine Parakeets always display shorter middle-tail feathers and thus shorter tails than adults. The adult feathering usually is acquired between 18–30 months of age, but may sometimes show up as young as 12 and/or as old as a full 36 months of age. Consequently, it may be difficult to identify the sex Alexandrine Parakeets by sight with absolute certainty until they are a full 36 months of age.

The young males can be identified as soon as they display one (or more) pitch-black feathers of their neck rings and/or one (or more) pink feathers of their nape bands. Often, the young males develop their neck rings and nape bands in two or sometimes three successive moulting seasons. Adult parakeets with neither pitch-black feathers in their neck rings nor pink feathers in their nape bands are usually females.

The *P. e. nipalensis* ssp. (Nepalese Alexandrine Parakeet) is the largest of the species measuring 62 cm (24.5 in) in total length with a wingspan averaging between 20–24 cm (8–9.5 in). It is thus recognized as the world's largest genuine Parakeet (short to mid sized *Long-Tailed* Parrot) species. It looks much like the Nominate sub-species. However, the feathers on the chest and abdomen in both genders display whitish-grey sheens, the cheeks and napes are washed with blue and the adult males display large pink nape bands.

The *P. e. magnirostris* ssp. (Andaman Island's Alexandrine Parakeet) is slightly larger than the nominate sub-species, displaying a wingspan anywhere between 20–22.5 cm (8–9 in). It looks much like the nominate race. However, the feathers on the chest and abdomen in both genders display whitish-grey sheens. The maroon 'shoulder' patch is of a much redder (or less brownish) colour than of that of the nominate. The beak is larger and more massive. The adult males display large pink nape bands, the blue sheens above the nape-bands are restricted and sometimes absent in some specimens.

The *P. e. avensis* ssp. (Indo-Burmese Alexandrine Parakeet) is of same size as the nominate species, also measuring 58 cm (23 in), displaying a wingspan averaging anywhere between 19.4–22 cm (7.5–8.5 in) and looks much like the Nominate ssp. However, the top of the head and the nape are of a yellowish-green, the blue sheens are restricted to the cheeks and thus absent in the nape. The adult males display thinner and pinker nape-bands.

The *P. e. siamensis* ssp. (Laos or Siamese Alexandrine Parakeet) is the smallest of the species, measuring 56 cm (22 in), displaying a wingspan averaging anywhere between 17.9–20.5 cm (7–8 in) and looks much like the Nominate ssp. However, the top of the head and the nape display pale-blue sheens that extends to the crown in some specimens. The cheeks are yellowish-green, the 'shoulder' patch is of a nearly brownless red colour and the legs display a pronounced yellowish shade.

Aviculture

The bird is popular among aviculturists. It is ideal for outdoor aviaries and is generally very hardy, however it cannot tolerate temperatures less than 5 °C (41 °F). They breed well in aviaries. The parakeet is one of the oldest captive Parakeet species on the Eurasian continent. It gets its name from the legendary Emperor Alexander The Great, who had numerous specimens exported back to various Mediterranean countries by his legionaries. The parakeet has since then been popular among the nobles throughout the Empire's Anatolian, European and Mediterranean countries.The species has naturalized (species that live and reproduce outside its natural distribution range) itself in numerous European countries. Particularly in Germany, in the south of England, in Belgium, in the Netherland where it generally lives amongst or along side flocks of naturalized Psittacula krameri.

Captivity

Male on cage

It is an active species, adventurous and curious, likes water (bathing, misting, raining and showering) and readily accepts diverse and/or new foods. It chews vigorously and hence it is important to keep the perch non-toxic without chemical products such as disinfectants, fungicide, insecticides or pesticides, and provide plenty of safe-to-chew toys. Alexandrines have very powerful beaks and enjoy the exercise of destroying wooden and plastic toys. The more toys you give the bird to chew, the less likely it will be to chew things it shouldn't. A bored Alexandrine is among the most potentially destructive creatures you can have in your home by weight. Alexandrines are very bright birds and take to reward-based training very well. They may be potty-trained very effectively and are quite willing to learn complex trick behaviors when rewarded with their favorite treats. When housing an Alexandrine care should be taken to make sure the cage is large enough that the bird can stand on a perch and fully stretch it's wings, and that there is enough room that the long tail featherrs are not constantly coming into contact with the bars of the cage. With their long tails and high activity levels Alexandrines require larger cages than many birds in their size class. When chosing a cage for any pet parrot, bigger is almost always better. The Alexandrine Parakeet has an average lifespan of 40 years in captivity and as with all other parakeets, they are among the top mimics.

Natural breeding habits

Breeding season is from November to April in their natural distribution range. Average clutch size is 2–4 eggs measuring 34.0 x 26.9 mm (1 x 1.3 in). The average incubation period is 28 days usually starting with the laying of the second egg. The chicks fledge around seven weeks of age. They are reared for about three weeks and are typically weaned between 12 to 16 weeks of age. They are critically endangered in Pakistan, especially in Punjab province. This is mostly due to loss of habitat, like cutting of old tress and excessive poaching of their new born chicks. Although it is officially banned in Pakistan to sell these parrots but they can be found openly being sold in markets of Lahore.Trapping pressure to cater to the demands of the pet trade have caused a drastic decline in this species. It is illegal to trade in Alexandrine Parakeets in India and yet these birds are sold in broad daylight in urban bird markets, suggesting that the Indian government is allocating insufficient resources towards the protection of this beautiful species.

Natural diet

The diet consists of seeds, nuts, fruits, berries, buds, flowers and nectars (Salmalia, Butea, Erythrina, Bassia latifolia). Rarely Alexandrines have been observed actively hunting insects, making them one of the few parrot species known to do so, however infrequently. It causes considerable damage to cultures of corn, grains, rice and orchards.

Diet in captivity

A fresh mix (with or without dehydrated fruits and/or vegetables) of various seeds, grains and nuts generally represent the typical basic diet. Many high-quality pelleted parrot foods are available and most Alexandrines will take to them readily. Pellets are generally nutritionally supeior to packaged seed mixes found in pet stores, and contain less fat. Alexandrines are not particularly prone to obesity, but high-fat diets may lead to fatty-liver disease, which can be fatal, and at the very least will lead to shortened life-span and reduced quality of life. Even when feeding a pelleted base diet, about 10% seed is appropriate. Variety is important both nutritionally and for your bird's enjoyment. Alexandrines are generally not picky eaters and will try almost anything once. Among the food items you can supplement the base diet with are: Cooked and fresh foods, whole grains and cereals, oatmeal, cooked pasta (in moderation), they enjoy edible blossoms and flowers, such as carnations, chamomile, chives, dandelion, daylily, eucalyptus, fruit tree's blossoms, herbs' blossoms, hibiscus, honeysuckle, impatiens, lilac, nasturtiums, pansies, passion flower (passifloræ), roses, sunflowers, tulips, and violets, fruits with all pits discarded, larger seeds such as apple varieties should also be removed. banana, all berries varieties, all citrus varieties, grapes, kiwi, mango, melons, nectarine, papaya, peach, all pear varieties, plum. Vegetables, such as carrot, squash, cooked yams, broccoli, cucumber, beetroot, turnip, etc. legumes/pulses and commercial greens and weeds such as bokchoi, broccoli, cauliflower leaves, cabbage leaves, chicory, collard greens, dandelion leaves, endives, espadrille, kelp, mustard plant leaves, seaweeds, spirulina and water cress. Wild harvested greens and weeds such as Bromus, chickweeds, cocksfoot or orchard grasses, dandelions, dogstooth, elymus, fescues, marram grasses, milk thistles, oats and wild oats, plantain (the weed), poa genus (i.e. Blue, Meadow's, Spear, Tussock grasses) may also be given. Well cooked poultry, pork and beef may be given in small quantities, as well as hard-cooked egg (with the shell mixed in), and active culture yogurts. High-protein foods should be fed more often during moulting and breeding. Generally if it is safe for humans to eat, then it is safe for parrots, with a few exceptions. Avocado and rhubarb are reportedly highly toxic for all Parrot species and should be avoided. Onions and large quantities of garlic may lead to anemia in parrots and intake of these should be limited, even though they are not immediately toxic. Parrots do not possess the needed enzymes to properly digest raw dairy products, and although many parrots love cheese and milk, intake should be limited. Avoid any foods that contain caffeine (including chocolate) and foods with high processed sugar content, and that are high in salt or contain sulfites. Birds should never be given alcohol. Alexandrines are social eaters and will appreciate any tidbits of bird-safe human food shared with them at meal times.

Gallery

Male at nest in Kolkata, West Bengal, India.

Alexandrine Parakeet flapping her wings

Male at nest in Kolkata, West Bengal, India.

Cultural depictions

Thailand, Mongolia and Iran have issued stamps depicting the Alexandrine Parakeet.

Source (edited): "http://en.wikipedia.org/wiki/Alexandrine_Parakeet"

American Mink

The **American mink** (*Neovison vison*) is a semi-aquatic species of Mustelid native to North America, though human intervention has expanded its range to many parts of Europe and South America. Because of this, it is classed as Least Concern by the IUCN. Since the extinction of the sea mink, the American mink is the only extant member of the genus *Neovison*. The American mink is a carnivore which feeds on rodents, fish, crustaceans, frogs and birds. In its introduced range in Europe, the American mink has been linked to declines in European mink and water vole. It is the most frequently farmed animal for its fur, outdoing in economic importance the silver fox, sable, marten and skunk.

Indigenous names
- **Cree**: *Sang-gwiss*, *Shakzuashew* or *Atjackasheiv*
- **Ojibwe**: *Shang-gwes'-se*
- **Chipewyan**: *Tel-chu'-say*
- **Ogallala Sioux**: *Lo-chin'-cha*
- **Yankton Sioux**: *Doke-sesch*

Evolution

As a species, the American mink represents a more specialised form than the European mink in the direction of carnivory, as indicated by the more developed structure of the skull. Fossil records of the American mink go back as far as the Irvingtonian, though the species is uncommon among Pleistocene animals. The fossil range of the American mink corresponds with the species' current natural range. The American minks of the Pleistocene did not differ much in size or morphology from modern populations, though a slight trend toward increased size is apparent from the Irvingtonian through to the Illinoian and Wisconsinan periods.

Although superficially similar to the European mink, studies indicate that the American mink's closest relative is the kolonok of Asia. The American mink has been recorded to hybridize with European minks and polecats in captivity, though the hybrid embryos of the American and European minks are usually reabsorbed.

Subspecies

As of 2005, 15 subspecies are recognised.

Physical description

Build

Skeleton of an American mink from the Muséum national d'histoire naturelle

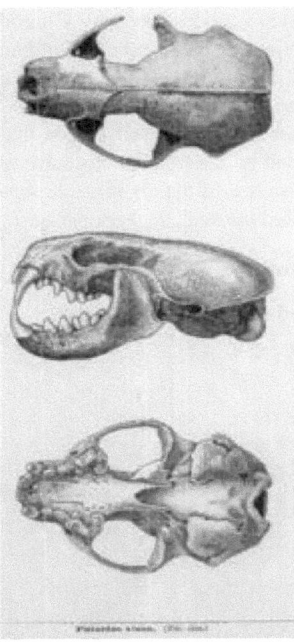

Skull as illustrated in Coues' *A monograph of North American Mustelidae*

The American mink differs from members of the genus *Mustela* (stoats and weasels) by its larger size and stouter form, which closely approaches that of martens. It shares with martens a uniformly enlarged, bushy and somewhat tapering tail, rather than a slenderly terete tail with an enlarged bushy tip, as is the case in stoats. The American mink is similar in build to the European mink, but the tail is longer (constituting 38-51% of its body length).

The American mink has a long body, which allows the species to enter the burrows of prey. Its streamlined shape helps it to reduce water resistance whilst swimming. The skull of the American mink is similar to that of the European mink, but is more massive, narrower and less elongated, with more strongly developed projections and a wider, shorter cranium. The upper molars are larger and more massive than those of the European mink. The dental formula is:

Domestic mink, which are bred in fur farms, have 19.6% smaller brains, 8.1% smaller hearts, and 28.2% smaller spleens than wild mink. The feet are broad, with webbed digits. It generally has eight nipples, with one pair of inguinal teats and three pairs of abdominal teats. The adult male's penis is 5.6 cm long, and is covered by a sheath. The baculum is well developed, being triangular in cross section and curved at the tip.

Males measure 34-45 cm in body length, while females measure 31-37.5 cm. The tail measures 15.6-24.7 cm in males and 14.8-21.5 cm in females. Weight varies with sex and season, with males being heavier than females. In winter, males weigh 500-1580 grams and females 400-780 grams. Maximum heaviness occurs in autumn.

American mink paws, as illustrated by Ernest Thompson Seton

Fur

The American mink's winter fur is denser, longer, softer and more close-fitting than that of the European mink. The winter fur's tone is generally very dark blackish-tawny to light-tawny Colour is evenly distributed over all the body, with the lower side being only slightly lighter than the upper body. The guard hairs are bright, dark-tawny, often approaching black on the spine. The underfur on the back is very wavy, greyish-tawny with a bluish tint. The tail is darker than the trunk and sometimes becomes pure black on the tip. The chin and lower lip are white. Captive individuals tend to develop irregular white patches on the lower surface of the body, though escaped individuals from Tartaria gradually lost these patches. The summer fur is generally shorter, sparser and duller than the winter fur. The thick underfur and oily guard hairs render the pelage water resistant, with the length of the guard hairs being intermediate between those of otters and polecats, thus indicating that the American mink is incompletely adapted to an aquatic life. It moults twice a year, during spring and autumn. It does not turn white in winter. A variety of different colour mutations have arisen from experimental breeding on fur farms.

Locomotion

On land, the American mink moves by a bounding gait, with speeds of up to 6.5 km/h. It also climbs trees and swims well. When diving, the American mink undergoes a state of rapid bradycardia, which is likely an adaptation to conserving oxygen. During swimming, the mink propels itself primarily through undulating movements of the trunk. In warm water (24°C), the American mink can swim for three hours without stopping, while in cold water it can die within 27 minutes. It generally dives to depths of 30 cm for 10 seconds, though depths of three metres lasting 60 seconds have been recorded. It typically catches fish after 5-20 second chases.

Senses and scent glands

The American mink relies heavily on sight when foraging. Its eyesight is clearer on land than underwater. Its auditory perception is high enough to detect the ultrasonic vocalisations (1-16 kHz) of rodent prey. Its sense of smell is comparatively weak. The American mink has two anal glands, which are used for scent marking, either through defecation or by rubbing the anal region on the ground. The secretions of the anal glands are composed of 2,2-dimethylthietane, 2-ethylthietane, cyclic disulfide, 3,3-dimethyl-1,2-dithiacyclopentane, and indole. When stressed, the American mink can expel the contents of its anal glands at a distance of 30 cm. Scent glands may also be located on the throat and chest. The smell produced by these scent glands was described by Clinton Hart Merriam as more unbearable than that produced by skunks, and added that it was "one of the few substances, of animal, vegetable, or mineral origin, that has, on land or sea, rendered me aware of the existence of the abominable sensation called *nausea*".

Behaviour

Social and territorial behaviours

A southern mink (*Neovison v. vulgivagus*) in a threatening posture

American mink in burrow

American mink territories are held by individual animals with minimal intrasexual overlap, but with extensive overlap between animals of the opposite sex. Most territories are located in undisturbed rocky coastal habitats with broad littoral zones and dense cover. They may also occur on estuaries, rivers and canals near urban areas. Home ranges are typically 1–6 km long, with male territories being larger than those of females. As long as it is close to water, the American mink is not fussy over its choice of den. Mink dens typically consist of long burrows in river banks, holes under logs, tree stumps or roots and hollow trees, though dens located in rock crevices, drains and nooks under stone piles and bridges are occasionally selected. Burrows dug by American minks themselves are typically about four inches in diameter and may be continue along for 10–12 feet at a depth of 2–3 feet. The American mink may nest in burrows dug previously by muskrats, badgers and skunks, and may also dig dens in old ant hills. The nesting chamber is located at the end of a four-inch tunnel, and is about a foot in diameter. It is warm, dry and lined with straw and feathers. The American mink's dens are characterized by a large number of entrances and twisting passages. The number of exits vary from 1-8.

The American mink normally only vocalises during close encounters with other minks or predators. Sounds emitted by the American mink include piercing shrieks and hisses when threatened and muffled chuckling sounds when mating. Kits squeak repeatedly when separated from their mothers. Ernest Thompson Seton reported hearing minks growl and snarl when confronting a threat. During aggressive interactions, the American mink asserts its dominance by arching its back, puffing up and lashing its tail, stamps and scrapes the ground with its feet and opens its mouth in a threat-gape. Should this be unsuccessful, fights may result, with injuries to the head and neck.

Reproduction and development

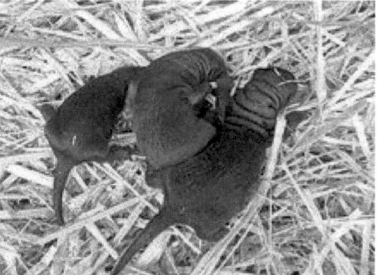

American mink kits

The American mink is a promiscuous animal, which does not form pair-bonds. The mating season for American minks begins from February in its southern range to April in the north. In its introduced range, the American mink breeds one month earlier than the European mink. Males commonly fight during the mating season, which may result in the formation of loose, temporary dominance hierarchies governing access to receptive females. The mating season lasts for three weeks, with ovulation being induced by the presence of males. The mating process in the American mink is violent, with the male typically biting the female on the nape of the neck and pinning her with his forefeet. Mating lasts from 10 minutes to four hours. Females are receptive for 7-10 day intervals during the three week breeding season, and can mate with multiple males. Along with the striped skunk, the American mink is among the only mammals to mate in spring whilst possessing a short delay before the occurrence of implantation. This delayed implantation allows pregnant minks to keep track of environmental conditions and select an ideal time and place for parturition.

The gestation period lasts from 40–75 days, with actual embryonic development taking place after 30–32 days, thus indicating that delayed implantation can last from 8–45 days. The young are born either in April or June, with litters consisting of four kits on average. Exceptionally large litters of 11 kits have been recorded in Tartaria and 16 in the United States. The kits are blind at birth, weighing six grams and possessing a short coat of fine, silver-white hairs. The kits are dependent on their mother's milk, which contains 3.8% lipids, 6.2% protein, 4.6% sugar and 10.66% mineral salts. Their eyes open after 25 days, with weaning occurring after five weeks. The kits begin hunting after eight weeks of age, but stay close to their mother until autumn, when they become independent. Sexual maturity is attained during the kit's first spring, when they are about 10 months old.

Diet

American mink with fish, in Norway

American mink with a salmon

The American mink is a carnivorous animal, which feeds on rodents, fish, crustaceans, amphibians and birds. It kills vertebrate prey by biting the back of the head or neck, leaving canine puncture marks 9–11 mm apart. In its natural range, fish are the American mink's primary prey. Although inferior to the North American river otter in hunting fish, Audubon and Bachman once reported seeing a mink carrying a foot-long trout. Mink inhabiting the prairie sloughs primarily target frogs, tadpoles, mice. It is a formidable predator of muskrats, which are chased underwater and killed in their own burrows. Among the rodents killed by the American mink in its native range are rats and mice of the genus *Hesperomys*, *Microtus*, *Sigmodon* and *Neotoma*. Marsh rabbits are frequently taken in marshy or swampy tracts.

In Tartaria, the American mink's most important food items are voles, fish, crustaceans, frogs and aquatic insects. In winter, aquatic foods predominate, while land-based prey increases in importance during the spring. Within the Altai Mountains, the American mink feeds predominantly on mammals such as rodents, shrews and moles, as well as birds, reptiles, amphibians and fish. Among the 11 different bird species preyed upon by minks in Altai are dippers and pine grosbeaks. Among fish, small species predominate in the diet of minks in Altai, and include minnows, gudgeons and wide-headed sculpins. In the Sverdlovsk and Irkutsk Oblasts, mouse-like rodents are the American mink's most important foods, followed by birds, fish and insects. In the Russian Far East, where crustaceans are scarce, the American mink feeds extensively on amphipods. In the British Isles, dietary composition varies seasonally and regionally. European rabbits are the most commonly taken prey in areas where they are common, especially in summer. A range of small rodents and insectivores are preyed upon, but to a lesser degree. European hares are occasionally attacked. Minks in Britain prey on several bird species, with ducks, moorhens and coots being most frequently targeted on lakes and rivers, while gulls are taken in coastal habitats. Aquatic species preyed upon in Britain include European eels, rock-pool fish such as blenny, shore crabs and crayfish. American Mink have been implicated in the decline of the water vole in the United Kingdom and linked to the decline of water fowl across their range in Europe. They are now considered vermin in much of Europe and are hunted for the purpose of wildlife management. In the Cape Horn Biosphere Reserve, mammals, including both native and exotic rodents, are the American mink's main prey throughout the year, though birds are of equal importance during their summer nesting period.

The American mink may pose a threat to poultry. According to Clinton Hart Merriam and Ernest Thompson Seton, although the American mink is a potential poultry thief, it is overall less damaging than the stoat. Unlike the stoat, which often engages in surplus killing, the mink usually limits itself to killing and eating one fowl during each attack. Studies in Britain indicate that poultry and game birds only constitute 1% of the animal's overall diet.

Relationships with other predators

The American mink replaces and sometimes kills the European mink wherever their ranges overlap. The decline of European mink populations seems to coincide with the spread of the American mink. The diets of the American mink and European otter overlap to a great extent. In areas where the two species are sympatric, competition with the otter for fish causes the American mink to hunt land-based prey more frequently.

Intelligence

An early behavioral study was performed in the 1960s that assessed visual learning ability in mink, ferrets, skunks, and house cats. Animals were tested on their ability to recognize objects, learn their valences and make object selections from memory. Mink were found to outperform ferrets, skunks and cats in this task, however this letter (short paper) fails to account for a possible conflation of a cognitive ability (decision making, associative learning) with a largely perceptual ability (invariant object recognition).

Range

Natural

The species' natural range encompasses North America from Alaska and Canada through the United States except Arizona and the more arid areas of California, Nevada, Utah, New Mexico, and western Texas.

Introduced

Mainland Europe and British Isles

An American mink being released from a fur farm in Rome by a member of the ALF

It is thought that feral American minks in Europe are of domesticated stock derived from the *vison, melampeplus* and *ingens* subspecies. The first specimens were imported to Europe in 1920 for fur-farming purposes. The American mink was introduced in Italy in the 1950s, and currently resides mostly in the northeastern part of the Italian Peninsula. The majority of these populations do not appear to be self sufficient, though minks in the Monti Prenestini and Simbruini in Lazio have reproduced successfully. The first mink farm in Norway was built in 1927, with escapees establishing wild populations within 30 years of its establishment. The first feral mink populations arose in 1930, establishing territories in southwestern Norway. These feral minks, augmented by further escapees, formed the basis of a strong population in Hordaland by the end of World War II. Feral mink colonised eastern Norway in 1930 and had become established in mosrt southeastern counties in the early 1940s. By 1950, feral mink reached central Norway, with further populations occurring in the northern counties of Nordland and Troms. During the post-World War II period up until 1965, mink had colonised most of the country. In modern times, the American mink occupies all of the Norwegian mainland, but is absent on some islands.

The American mink was first imported to Great Britain in 1929, though a series of escapes and releases lead to the establishment of a self-sufficient feral population in Devon by the late 1950s, and others by the early 1960s. In Ireland, the American mink was not farmed until the early 1950s, thus feral populations established themselves there much later. The species is now widespread in mainland Great Britain and Ireland, though some places remain uncolonised. It has established itself on a few islands, including Arran, Lewis and Harris. The total mink population in Great Britain is estimated at 110,000 (England; 46,750, Scotland; 52,250, Wales; 9750). This population may be declining as European otter numbers increase. There are no estimates for the mink population in Ireland, but it is thought to be low, because of Ireland's strong otter population.

Former USSR

An American mink in Lithuania's Kėdainiai district

In 1933, American minks were released into the Voronezh Oblast in European Russia. Until 1963, more minks were introduced in various quantities in the Voronezh and Arkhangelsk Oblasts, Karelia, in Kalininsk, Gorkovsk, Volgograd and Chelyabinsk Oblasts, and into Tatarstan and Bashkir, as well as the Lithuanian and Byelorussian SSRs. Beyond the Urals, American minks were introduced in the Sverdlovsk, Tyumen, Omsk, Kemerovo, Novosibirsk, Chita and Irkutsk Oblasts, in the Altai and Krasnoyarsk Krai, in the Tuvan, Buryat and Yakut Autonomous Soviet Socialist Republics, into the Magadan, Kamchatka and Amur Oblasts, into the Khabarovsk and Primorsky Krai, into the Chukotka Autonomous Okrug and several other locations, including Sakhalin and Urup Island. In the Caucasus, American mink were released into North Ossetia and Tien Shan. Originally, captive-bred mink were used, but wild specimens were later released in order to facilitate the species' acclimatisation within Soviet territories. Several years after the first release, introductions into the ranges already held by native European minks were discontinued, with most releases from then on taking place in Siberia and the Far East. Although considerable areas were occupied by the American mink by the early 1960s, the species' Soviet range was never continuous, as most released populations were isolated from one another.

Iceland

The species has been present in Iceland since the 1930s, and has become well established, despite it being heavily hunted since 1939. However, its population underwent a 42% decline during the years 2002-2006, which coincided with a decline in sandeel populations resulting in a drop in the seabird populations which the minks feed upon.

South America

The American mink was deliberately introduced for commercial fur production in several provinces of Patagonia in 1930. The animals escaped or were released from farms in Chubut Province and now occur in the Chubut and Río Negro Provinces and Tierra del Fuego.

Diseases and parasites

The American mink often carries light tick and flea infestations. Tick species known to infest minks include *Ixodes hexagonus*, *I. canisuga*, *I. ricinus* and *I. acuminatus*. Flea species known to infest minks include *Palaeopsylla minor*, *Malaraeus penicilliger*, *Ctenopthalmus noblis*, *Megabothris walkeri*, *Typhloceras poppei* and *Nosopsyllus fasciatus*. Endoparasites include *Skrjabingylus nasicola* and *Troglotrema acutum*.

Transmissible mink encephalopathy (TME) is a prion disease of mink, similar to BSE in cattle and scrapie in sheep. A 1985 outbreak of TME in Stetsonville, Wisconsin resulted in a 60% mortality rate for the mink. Further testing revealed that this agent is transmissible between mink, cattle and sheep. The Stetsonville outbreak may have been due to the animals being fed the carcasses of other infected animals.

Decline of wild mink

Because of numerous incidents of domestic mink escaping from fur farms and establishing themselves in the wild, concern has arisen among conservationists of the possible repercussions such escapes may have on natural wild mink populations. Domestic mink are larger than wild mink, which may cause problems with the ecosystem when they escape. Mink are solitary, territorial animals and are intolerant of other mink. In times of overpopulation, mink control their own numbers by either killing each other through direct conflict or by causing weaker mink to be driven from territory until starvation sets in. When hundreds or thousands of released domestic mink flood an ecosystem, it causes a great disturbance for the wild mink, resulting in the deaths of the majority of the released mink and many of the wild mink from starvation or injuries incurred fighting over territory. When a domestic mink survives long enough to reproduce, it may cause problems for the wild mink populations. The adding of weaker domestic mink genes into wild mink populations is believed by some to have contributed to the decline of mink populations in Canada.

A 2006 study in Denmark concluded that, due to frequent escapes from existing mink farms, "Closing mink farms may result in a crash of the free-ranging population, or alternatively it may result in the establishment of a better-adapted, truly feral population that may ultimately outnumber the population that was present before farm closures." The study reported that more information would be necessary to determine the outcome. Another Danish study reported that a significant majority of the "wild" mink were mink which had escaped from fur farms. 47% had escaped within two months, 31% had escaped prior to 2 months, and 21% "may or may not have been born in nature." The survival rate for recently released mink is reportedly lower than for wild mink, but if feral mink survive at least two months, their survival rate is the same as for wild mink. The authors suggest that this is due to the rapid behavioural adaptation of the animals.

Relationships with humans

Fur use

American mink are primarily used in manufacturing ladies' fur coats, jackets and capes. Pelts which are not able to be converted into these items are made into trimming for cloth and fur coats. Mink scarves and stoles are also manufactured. Jackets and capes are mostly made from small to medium-sized specimens, usually females and young males, while trimming, scarves and stoles are made from adult males. The most valuable peltries come from eastern Canada which, although the smallest, are the silkiest and darkest.

Trapping

Illustration of an American mink approaching a board or log trap

Although difficult to catch, the American mink, prior to being commercially farmed, was among the most frequently trapped furbearers as, unlike other furbearing mammals, it did not hibernate in winter, and could thus be caught on a nightly basis even in the far north. Minks were legally trapped from early November to early April, when their pelts were prime. Minks caught in traps cling to life with great tenacity, having been known to break their teeth in trying to extricate themselves from steel traps. Elliott Coues described a trapped mink as thus ;

One who has not taken a Mink in a steel trap can scarcely form an idea of the terrible expression the animal's face assumes as the captor approaches. It has always struck me as the most nearly diabolical of anything in animal physiognomy. A sullen stare from the crouched, motionless form gives way to a new look of surprise and fear, accompanied with the most violent contortions of the body, with renewed champing of the iron till breathless, with heaving flanks, and open mouth dribbling saliva, the animal settles again, and watches with a look of concentrated hatred, mingled with impotent rage and frightful despair. The countenance of the Mink, its broad, low head, short ears, small eyes, piggish snout, and formidable teeth, is always expressive of the lower and more brutal passions, all of which are intensified at such times. As may well be supposed, the creature must not be incautiously dealt with when in a such a frame of mind.

—

One Native American method involved using a bait (usually a slit open chicken carcass filled with fish oil and oysters) tied to a rope and dragged around an area laden with traps. A mink would thus follow the trail into one of the traps. Another indigenous method involved placing traps scented with muskrat and female mink musk on top of disused muskrat dens by water-bodies. Attracted by the scent of food and a female, the mink would get caught in the trap and drown. On the American prairies, only the steel trap was used, because of the lack of timber.

Farming

Various American mink colour mutations

Breeding American mink for their fur began in the late 19th century, as increasing enthusiasm for mink pelts made the harvesting of wild mink insufficient to meet the new demands. American mink are easily kept in captivity, and breed readily. In 2005, the U.S. ranked fourth in production behind Denmark, China and the Netherlands. Mink typically breed in March, and give birth to their litters in May. Farmers vaccinate the young kits for botulism, distemper, enteritis, and, if needed, pneumonia. They are harvested in late November and December. Methods for killing animals on fur farms, as on all farms, are detailed in the American Veterinary Medical Association's Report on Euthanasia which is used as a voluntary guideline for state departments of agriculture which have jurisdiction over all farms raising domesticated livestock, including mink. Successful mink-farms have pools of water for the mink to swim in. The ideal diet for farm-bred minks consists of 4-5 ounces of horse meat and a quarter pint of milk once daily.

Colour mutations

Selective breeding has produced a number of different colour shades in mink peltries, ranging from pure white, through beiges and browns and greys, to a brown that is almost black. The two standard strains are brown and "Black cross" which, when paired, produce numerous colour variations. When an albino mink is born, it is standard procedure in fur farms to breed it to other colour mutations in order to produce grey and light brown pastel shades. The following graph is a simplification of the main colour strains;

As pets

Mink as pet

Wild mink can be tamed if caught young, but can be treacherous, and are usually not handled bare-handed. In the late 19th century, tame American minks were often reared for ratting, much as ferrets were used in Europe. They are more effective ratters than terriers, as they can enter rat-holes and drive rats from their hiding places. Because of their fondness for bathing, captive American minks may enter kettles or other open water-containing vessels. When minks of wild stock are confined with tame ones, the latter invariably dominate the former. They have also been known to dominate cats in confrontations. Though intelligent, mink are not quick to learn tricks taught to them by their owners. Even though domestic mink have been bred in captivity for almost a century, they have not been bred to be tame. Domestic mink have been bred for size, fur quality, and color. However, the US Fur Commission claims that "mink are truly domesticated animals" based on the number of years they have been kept on fur farms. Source (edited): "http://en.wikipedia.org/wiki/American_Mink"

Arapawa Sheep

Arapawa ram

The **Arapawa Sheep** is a breed of feral sheep found primarily on Arapawa Island in the Marlborough Sounds, New Zealand, where they have probably been isolated since they were introduced in 1867. Although there are many theories of how the sheep arrived, it is generally accepted that they are descendents of Merino strains from Australia. The New Zealand Rare Breeds Conservation Society classifies this breed as "rare". This breed is raised primarily for wool.

Characteristics

Ewes have no horns, but rams have long spiral horns that often measure over 1 metre (3 ft). The fiber is of Merino-like fineness.

Due to living in a rather hostile and very steep terrain, this breed often looks hunched over as they carry their head and tail down most often. They have a light build and long legs making them a rather active breed. The head and face are narrow and clear while the ears are slender. They are naturally resistant to fly strike—a characteristic that would be beneficial in commercial flocks.

Most often, the Arapawa displays all black. However, quite often, white points are displayed. On rare occasions, an all white sheep can be observed. "Cocktail" Arapawas are those that are white spotted.

Source (edited): "http://en.wikipedia.org/wiki/Arapawa_Sheep"

Australian feral camel

The ancestors of **Australian feral camels** were dromedary camels imported to provide transport through inland Australia, which their feral descendants have since made their home. The increasing numbers of camels and their impact on native vegetation is of concern, and feral camels have become minor agricultural pests.

Many different types and breeds of camels were brought into Australia, but most were from India. They included the large, fleece-bearing, two-humped Bactrian camel of China and Mongolia, the elite Bishari riding camel of North Africa and Arabia, the pedigreed Bikaneri war camel of Rajasthan in India, and the powerful, freight-carrying lowland Indian camel, capable of moving huge loads of up to 800 kg or 1,764 lb.

The feral dromedary camels found in Australia are a mix of these breeds but can be split into two types: a slender riding form and a heavier pack animal.

Thousands of camels were imported between 1840 and 1907 to open up the arid areas of central and western Australia. They were used for riding, and as draught and pack animals for exploration and construction of rail and telegraph lines; they were also used to supply goods to remote mines and settlements.

Camels in Australia are the only feral herds of their kind in the world, and are estimated to number more than 1,000,000, with the capability of doubling in number every nine years. The Australian camels are descendants of camels imported into Australia, beginning in the mid-19th century, to help lay the foundations of the nation. Shipments came largely from the Indian subcontinent, but animals were also landed from Muscat, Yemen, Iraq and the Canary Islands.

Arriving in a trickle that swelled to a flood by the early 20th century, the camels were often guided and cared for by Muslim cameleers known as 'Afghans'. Handlers came from lands as far away as Egypt, Turkey and Persia, though most — with their camels — hailed from northern India and what today is Pakistan. But the men were all, almost always incorrectly, called Afghans or simply "Ghans." The name stuck to a section of the 2,900 km (1,800 mi) transcontinental Central Australia Railway linking Port Augusta in the south to Darwin in the north. Camels hauled material and supplies to the men building that line beginning in 1879, and the segment of track from Port Augusta to Alice Springs was called "The Ghan" until it was relaid near the end of the 20th century.

It could be argued that the town of Alice Springs owes its existence to the hardy camel and the equally hardy cameleers. It was founded in the early 1870s as a repeater station for the Darwin-to-Adelaide Overland Telegraph Line — which was also built by men who depended on dromedaries for supplies and equipment. Plodding camels not only helped establish "The Alice," they brought it music: The first piano arrived in the 1880s, the story goes, strapped to the back of a camel Aptly, the city holds a state legislative district, a primary school and a major thoroughfare all named after cameleer Saleh "Charlie" Sadadeen, who came to Alice Springs with his team in 1890 "Children were enthralled with his distinctive, flowing robes and intrigued with the long-stemmed pipe he smoked," reports the *Alice Springs Centralian Advocate*.

Men like Sadadeen came to Australia on two- to three-year contracts but often lived out their lives in the country writes American geographer Tom McKnight in *The Camel in Australia*

While a handful became wealthy, deploying "thousands of camels organized into the backbone of corporate business," most toiled from dawn to well past dusk for low pay, and lived near outback towns in little communities distinguished by the "tin minarets of their hastily constructed mosques." Wherever the cameleers settled, writes McKnight, "they would soon construct a place of worship. In every case the mosque was a focal point of community life in Ghan Town."

The first camel

The first suggestion of bringing camels to Australia was made in 1822 by Conrad Malte-Brun, whose *Universal Geography* contains the following;
"For such an expedition, men of science and courage ought to be selected. They ought to be provided with all sorts of implements and stores, and with different animals, from the powers and instincts of which they may derive assistance. They should have oxen from Buenos Aires, or from the English settlements, mules from Senegal, and dromedaries from Africa or Arabia. The oxen would traverse the woods and the thickets; the mules would walk securely among rugged rocks and hilly countries; the dromedaries would cross the sandy deserts. Thus the expedition would be prepared for any kind of territory that the interior might present. Dogs also should be taken to raise game, and to discover springs of water; and it has even been proposed to take pigs, for the sake of finding out esculent roots in the soil. When no kangaroos and game are to be found the party would subsist on the flesh of their own flocks. They should be provided with a balloon for spying at a distance any serious obstacle to their progress in particular directions, and for extending the range of observations which the eye would take of such level lands as are too wide to allow any heights beyond them to come within the compass of their view."

The first serious Australian suggestion for using camels was 1837 when Governor Bourke of New South Wales received a report recommending the importation of camels from India to Sydney. The *Sydney Herald* took up the call, arguing that camels were "admirably adapted to the climate and soil" of the unexplored country. Though it was not until the 1860s that dromedaries were brought to Australia in any numbers, the first camel — named "Harry" — arrived in 1840, the sole survivor of a group of four loaded aboard the SS *Appoline* at Tenerife in the Canary Islands. Though they would soon prove vital to the country's development, their first representative hardly set a good example.

On a surveying expedition to the Lake Torrens area of South Australia in 1846, Harry bit the tentkeeper, grabbed a goat by the back of the neck and "chewed a hole in a bag of flour, leaving a white trail along the route," according to an account of the journey. But the straw that broke Harry's back came when he bumped his owner, John Horrocks, just as Horrocks was reloading his muzzle-loader with fine shot to take a bird as a scientific specimen. Horrocks lost two fingers and several teeth in the ensuing blast, and died a month later of gangrene. The camel was shot at his express wish, not as revenge, but because Harry was clearly a bad specimen who would give camels as a whole a bad name.

In May 1841, between Harry's arrival and his premature death, two female camels acquired from the Imam of Muscat arrived in Sydney via India aboard the SS *Malta* — the fourth and fifth dromedaries to reach Australia. (The second and third were from Tenerife and landed in Hobart, Tasmania from the SS *Calcutta*, but there is no record of what happened to them). A male companion from Muscat had died en route. Seeking buyers, the animals' importer, Captain John Martin Ardlie (1793–1872), took the camels from Sydney to Melbourne, but despite the *Herald*'s counsel, no one was interested in purchasing them. Ardlie returned the camels to Sydney where Governor Gipps bought the animals, along with a replacement male, and ordered them to be pastured on the Sydney Domain. Two were painted nibbling on the lawn there in 1845, and the painting is held at the Mitchell Library.

The camel as a beast of burden

Burke, Wills and King arrive at Cooper's Creek by John Longstaff

In 1860, the camel was first called on to do the work for which it was ideally suited: long-distance exploration in a continent of some 7,000,000 km (2,700,000 sq mi). But here, too, first results were far from promising. Twenty-six camels, several originally imported from Aden in 1859 to perform in a show in Melbourne, were included in the 20-man, 23-horse Burke and Wills expedition that set off from Melbourne in August 1860 in a bid to cross the unmapped continent from south to north. A picked team of four men, six camels and a single horse made the last 1,600 km (990 mi) push from a base camp at Cooper Creek, reaching the north coast in February 1861. But none of those camels — and only one man, John King — made it back. Of the six camels who crossed Australia, two were eaten, two abandoned and two destroyed when they became too tired to continue.

Instead, the relief mission that departed from Adelaide under John McKinlay in 1862 first proved the value of camels in rough terrain — for a novel reason. McKinlay never found Burke and Wills but did return with valuable reconnaissance, and he praised his camels for their ability to move over stones and through muddy, flooded country. "The camels acted famously," he wrote, "... from their great height they were as good [in protecting the expedition's stores] as if we had been supplied with boats." Further camel-mounted expeditions helped unlock the secrets of the vast, arid interior in the 1870s, pushing through South Australia and Western Australia and what from 1909 became the Northern Territory. Indeed, the first Europeans to set eyes on magnificent Uluru (Ayers Rock), the 350 m (1,150 ft) sandstone monolith on the central Australian plain, were the members of the camel-borne 1873 William Gosse Expedition. The 1894 Horn Expedition to the MacDonnell Ranges used camels for transport of people and equipment.

Camel train transporting a house, Kalgoorlie, Western Australia, c. 1928.

Australia's first large-scale camel importer was Scottish-born Sir Thomas Elder, whose interest in dromedaries can probably be traced to his own experience in the Middle East. Nine years after an 1857 camel journey from Cairo to Jerusalem, Elder started a stud farm about 400 km (250 mi) north of Port Augusta, with 121 camels shipped in from Karachi. That first shipment, chosen with care to meet a variety of outback needs, included light camels for riding, medium-weight pack animals and heavy Kandahar dromedaries able to carry loads up to 650 kg (1,400 lb). Elder's enterprise wasn't trouble-free as his herd was immediately struck by mange and reduced by almost half. But with the animals that remained, supplemented by additional imports, he produced carefully bred beasts that consistently brought higher prices than any others, home-grown or imported. With Elder leading the way, Australian camel importers began to buy in earnest as the 19th century drew to a close. Between 1894 and 1897 6,000 camels were shipped from India directly to Western Australia, mainly to serve the booming gold camps. In 1910, there were more than 8,400 camels in the country. Numbers peaked around 1920 with some 20,000 in harness.

The firm Elder founded continues today as Elders Limited, and even though it long ago phased out its camel trade, it has retained an interest in the animals — the company supplied ten camels for a 3,426 km (2,129 mi), 117-day walk from Darwin to Adelaide by the Northern Territory and South Australia police forces. The expedition's arrival on 1 January 1988 was timed to kick off Australia's bicentennial celebrations. In 1986, Elder also aided a central Australian Aboriginal community trying to sell several thousand camels to the Moroccan government.

Camels were able to carry heavy loads over long distances and go for days without a drink, they proved better adapted than horses or bullocks to working in a continent half of which is arid or semi-arid and where summertime temperatures often soar beyond 48 °C (118 °F).

Camels did a variety of important jobs. They hauled the casings that lined the wells that tapped underground water, which opened wide areas to the livestock industry vital to the Australian economy to this day. They carried the fencing — and later the fence riders — that held back rabbits from the newly opened ranges; they lugged supplies to sheep stations and mines and returned with bales of wool and wagonloads of ore; they dragged scoops to carve out lake basins; they pulled passenger coaches between towns where there was barely a road; and they transported policemen and postmen on their appointed rounds far from cities or towns. Outback journeymen even found that the trails pounded smooth by the padded feet of hundreds of dromedaries made excellent routes for bicycling hundreds of kilometres between jobs.

The early camels weren't dawdlers, either. In a famous race between a camel and a horse, completed between Bourke and Wanaaring in New South Wales and back again, the camel mount of Abdul Wadi (1866-1928+) won when the horse died from exhaustion at the half-way mark. Abdul Wadi proudly rode his camel to the finish.

Today camel races are popular, and include the annual Imparja Camel Cup raced with up to 15 camels At Blatherskite Park in Alice Springs and the Boulia Desert Sands Camel Cup.

Decline in use and rise as a pest

At their zenith, dromedaries were in use in some three-quarters of the continent. What is more, in a bit of irony that Sir Thomas Elder might have relished, the Australian Camel Corps even served in Egypt and Palestine in World War I as part of Great Britain's Imperial Camel Corps. The force consisted of three companies of Australian Camel Corps to one British, and a company of Hong Kong artillery. But by the middle of the 1920s the future was looking cloudy for Australian cameleers and camel ranchers — clouded by the choking waves of red dust sent up by automobiles and trucks, the new wave of imports into the outback. From the 1930s on, in all but a few long-distance, off-road cases, the camel was a museum piece.

Camel men watched the value of their stock plummet, but the feral camel thrived in the bush: Recent surveys show wide camel ranges extending from the Northern Territory and South Australia in the centre of the continent well into Western Australia, with animals also reported in the northeastern state of Queensland. The Northern Territory Parks and Wildlife Commission estimated a population of more than one million in 2009, expected to double in nine years, jeopardising cattle pastures. With no natural predators to control the spread of wild camels, the population grows around 10% each year.

Australia boasts the largest population of feral camels and the only herd of dromedary (one-humped) camels exhibiting wild behaviour in the world. (Other feral dromedary populations existed in the 20th century in Doñana National Park in Spain, and in the southwestern United States, while a small population of wild Bactrian camels still exists in the Gobi Desert.) Live camels are exported to Saudi Arabia, the United

Arab Emirates, Brunei and Malaysia, where disease-free wild camels are prized as a delicacy. Australia's camels are also exported as breeding stock for Arab camel racing stables and for use in tourist venues in places such as the United States.

Impact on the environment

It has been suggested that the camel is an ecological replacement for the now-extinct Diprotodon, as the dingo was to the Thylacine (commonly known as the Tasmanian Tiger), in Australia.

Although their impact on the environment is not as severe as some other pests introduced in Australia, camels feed on more than 80% of the available plant species. Degradation of the environment occurs when densities exceed two animals per km, which is presently the case throughout much of their range in the Northern Territory where they are confined to two main regions: the Simpson Desert and fringing pastoral properties, and the western desert area comprising the Central Ranges, Great Sandy Desert and Tanami Desert. Some traditional food plants harvested by Aboriginal people in these areas are seriously affected by camel browsing. While having soft-padded feet makes soil erosion less likely, feral camels do have a noticeable impact on salt lake ecosystems, foul waterholes and destabilise dune crests, which contributes to erosion.

The significant damage that camels have done, and are currently doing, to the fragile ecosystems, cultural sites, isolated communities, and pastoral enterprises of desert Australia has gone largely unnoticed by the bulk of Australia's population.

Effect on infrastructure

The effects on built infrastructure may be severe, as camels may sometimes destroy taps, pumps and even toilets as a means to obtain water, particularly in times of severe drought. They also damage stock fences and cattle watering points. These effects are felt particularly in Aboriginal and other remote communities where the costs of repairs is prohibitive. The problem with invading camels searching for water has become great enough that the Australian authorities have planned to eradicate as many as 6,000 camels that have become a nuisance in the community of Docker River, where the camels have caused severe damages in their search for food and water.

Source (edited): "http://en.wikipedia.org/wiki/Australian_feral_camel"

Burmese Pythons in Florida

The Burmese python, a large, non-venomous constrictor native to Southeast Asia, has been sighted and captured with increasing frequency in the Everglades and is generally labeled an invasive species. Their range is expanding, though the eventual limits are still disputed, and efforts are underway to control or eradicate them.

Timeline

While isolated individuals, probably recent releases or escapees, have been reported since the 1980s, the numbers captured since 2000 have shown a dramatic increase. However, the increase in python captures in the Everglades may be due to an increase in search effort in recent years. A severe winter in early 2010 is believed to have killed a large number of the snakes, but there are currently no publications suggesting this significantly reduced the overall population. The incident has brought in to question the possibility of cold snaps helping to propagate a more cold-resistant population by weeding out less cold-hardy individuals. 2011 also produced evidence of cold-killed Burmese pythons, and the largest snakes appear to be most vulnerable.

Origin

While the origin of this snake in the Everglades is unknown, blame has fallen on pet owners thought to have abandoned the snakes once they reached unmanageable sizes. An alternative theory states that a specific holding warehouse filled with newly imported Burmese pythons was destroyed by Hurricane Andrew, releasing the snakes en masse in a single area. Genetic studies using mitochondrial DNA and microsatellite genotyping have only been able to determine that the population in Everglades National Park is not genetically structured which could be explained by several hypotheses.

Eventual range

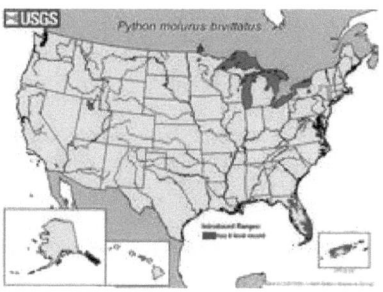

Current US range.

In February 2008, USGS scientists published a projected range map for the US, based on average climate data of the snake's home range and global warming projections, which predicted that these snakes could eventually migrate to and flourish in as much as a third of the continental United States by the end of the 21st century. Live studies of snakes at the Savannah River Ecology lab indicate an intolerance of below freezing weather, as all snakes released died over the winter. This draws into contention the validity of the USGS report, with many critics citing the very limited number of variables utilized by Gordon

Rodda et al when the map was created.

Wind Chill Factor

A subsequent study produced a map incorporating both climatic extremes and averages, which showed the Burmese python's range to be limited to Southern Florida.

Ecological interactions

An American Alligator preying on a Burmese Python. Photo by Lori Oberhofer, National Park Service.

Burmese pythons captured in the everglades have been found with a wide variety of mammals and birds in their stomachs, including endangered species and even small alligators. Alligators have been observed preying upon pythons. In October 2005, Everglades National Park Rangers, (USA), had discovered the carcass of a 6-foot (1.8 meter) American Alligator protruding from the burst and headless body of 13-foot (4 meter) Burmese python. It was suggested that a third animal or human was responsible for cutting open and decapitating the snake.

Control

A skin-hunting season was planned by the Florida Fish and Wildlife Conservation Commission and took place in the Everglades between March 8 and April 17, 2010 in hopes of reducing the snake's numbers. Other proposed methods include trapping and tracking radio-tagged snakes.

Legislative Response

Senator Bill Nelson has introduced S. 373 to the US Senate, the bill that bans the snakes from being imported into America as well as inter-state trade, while the Florida legislature has tightened restrictions on the ownership of existing animals within the state. The Florida bill came into effect July 1, 2010, while S. 373 died. Other bills attempting to limit the trade in large constrictors have since been proposed. This has prompted a backlash among members of the reptile trade industry, who feel that the very limited potential range of large constrictors in the US does not warrant banning trade throughout the country.

Source (edited): "http://en.wikipedia.org/wiki/Burmese_Pythons_in_Florida"

Campbell Island sheep

Campbell Island sheep are a feral breed of domestic sheep formerly found on Campbell Island, New Zealand.

History

The sheep farmers

The sheep were originally introduced to Campbell Island in the late 1890s, following the inclusion of the island in New Zealand's pastoral lease system in 1896. The lease was first taken up by James Gordon of Gisborne, who shipped 400 sheep, along with timber for buildings, to the island. After financial difficulties, in 1900 the lease was bought out by Captain Tucker of the Gisborne Militia who stocked the island with at least three shipments of about 1,000 sheep, mainly merino or merino cross. Two businessmen from Otago, J. Mathewson and D. Murray, became the next lessees in 1916, forming the Campbell Island Company (later a Syndicate) to manage the farm, employing shepherds and shearers to work for one-year periods on the island.

In 1927 the lease was auctioned and bought by John Warren, a farmer from Waitati, who brought another 5000 sheep to the island. However, wool and meat prices slumped in 1929 and, two years later, a destitute Warren and his farm workers returned to the mainland, abandoning the farm and the sheep. The lease to the island was declared forfeit in 1934 and expired in 1937. That year the island was set aside for the preservation of its flora and fauna, though its gazettal as a nature reserve did not take place until 1954.

The sheep

With an initial abundance of palatable food, sheep numbers increased to a peak in about 1913 of 7-8000. Gradually, as the palatable plants became eaten out, the population went into a decline, with the flock down to 4000 in 1931 when it was abandoned. In 1958 a count of the sheep found about 1000 remaining.

However, there was some subsequent recovery in numbers. In 1970 a fence was built across the island with all 1300 sheep on the northern side being shot, with a similar number on the southern side being left for the time being. By the late 1980s all the remaining sheep were culled, after a rescue expedition in 1975/76 removed ten live sheep for captive breeding in New Zealand. Descendants of the rescued sheep were maintained as a purebred flock until 2005.

Source (edited): "http://en.wikipedia.org/wiki/Campbell_Island_sheep"

Canadian Parliamentary Cats

Thumbelina, one of the strays.

The **Parliamentary Cats** are a collection of stray cats living in the precinct of Parliament Hill in Ottawa, Ontario. A small colony on the grounds, called the Cat Sanctuary, is set aside for them. The care of the cats and maintenance of the sanctuary is carried out by volunteers, and the effort is funded purely by donation.

Caretakers

Cats were employed in the Parliament Building to control the rodent population until 1955 when they were replaced by chemicals. Groundskeepers fed the cats at various locations on the grounds until the 1970s. In the late 1970s, Irène Desormeaux began feeding the cats at the location of the current colony. She was joined by René Chartrand in the mid-1980s

Chartrand took over when Desormeaux died in 1987. Chartrand received the Heroes for Animals Award from the Humane Society of Canada for his work in 2003. One of his contributions was the construction of shelters in the colony.

Brian Caines and Klaus Gerken established a volunteer team in 2003 to aid Chartrand, and later assumed total responsibility when Chartrand retired in 2009.

A list of volunteers may be found on this site.

The Colony

The colony is located west of the Centre Block and the statue of Alexander Mackenzie. The fence surrounding the colony is no obstacle to the cats and they are free to roam the grounds.

Chartrand built the first set of cold weather shelters in the mid-1980s, some of which are still extant. The current structures, resembling the houses of European settlers along the St. Lawrence, were built by Chartrand and a friend in 1997.

While formally intended for the cats, raccoons, groundhogs, pigeons and squirrels also partake in the cats' benefits.

In 2003, the estimated annual cost of the colony was C$6000.

Cats

The cats are spayed or neutered, and receive free inoculations and care, from the local Alta Vista Animal Hospital. Purina also donates food.

In 2003, there were approximately 30 cats. However, once spaying and neutering occurred the population slowly dropped off until there were no more than a dozen cats present at any one time.

A list of current permanent and prior residents may be found on this site.

Gallery

Cats napping outside their house.

René Chartrand caring for the cats.

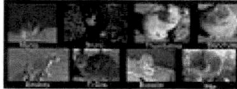
Portraits of several of the cats.

The sanctuary as seen from the grounds. Source (edited): "http://en.wikipedia.org/wiki/Canadian_Parliamentary_Cats"

Donkey

The **donkey** or **ass**, *Equus africanus asinus*, is a domesticated member of the Equidae or horse family. The wild ancestor of the donkey is the African Wild Ass, *E. africanus*. In the western United States, a small donkey is sometimes called a *burro* (from the Spanish word for the animal).

A male donkey or ass is called a **jack**, a female a jenny, and an offspring less than one year old a foal (male: colt, female: filly).

While different species of the Equidae family can interbreed, offspring are almost always sterile. Nonetheless, horse/donkey hybrids are popular for their durability and vigor. A mule is the offspring of a jack (male donkey) and a mare (female horse). The much rarer successful mating of a male horse and a female donkey produces a hinny.

Asses were first domesticated around 3000 BC, approximately the same time as the horse, and have spread around the world. They continue to fill important roles in many places today. While domesticated species are increasing in numbers, the African wild ass and another relative, the Onager, are endangered. As "beasts of burden" and companions, asses and donkeys have worked together with humans for millennia.

Scientific and common names

Traditionally, the scientific name for the donkey is *Equus asinus asinus* based on the principle of priority used for scientific names of animals. However, the International Commission on Zoological Nomenclature ruled in 2003 that if the domestic species and the wild species are considered subspecies of each other, the scientific name of the wild species has priority, even when that subspecies was described after the domestic subspecies. This means that the proper scientific name for the donkey is *Equus africanus asinus* when it is considered a subspecies, and *Equus asinus* when it is considered a species.

Until recently the synonym *ass* was the more common term for the donkey, as in *jackass*, meaning "male donkey". The first written use of *donkey* is as recent as 1785. While the word *ass* has cognates in most other Indo-European languages, *donkey* is an etymologically obscure word for which no credible cognate has been identified. Hypotheses on its derivation include the following:
- Perhaps a diminutive of *dun* (dull grayish-brown), a typical donkey colour.
- Perhaps from the name *Duncan*.
- Perhaps of imitative origin.

The homonymity in the United States with a vulgar term *ass* for "buttocks" may have influenced its gradual replacement by *donkey* there, though this does not account for the parallel change in Britain and Australia.

Characteristics

Donkeys vary considerably in size, depending on breed and management. The height at the withers ranges from 80 to 160 cm (31 to 63 in), and the weight from 80 to 480 kg (180 to 1060 lb). Donkeys have a lifespan of 30 to 50 years.

Donkeys are adapted to marginal desert lands, and have many traits that are unique to the species as a result. Wild donkeys live separated from each other, unlike tight wild horse and feral horse herds. Donkeys have developed very loud vocalizations, which help keep in contact with other donkeys over the wide spaces of the desert. The best-known call is referred to as a "bray," which can be heard for over three kilometers. Donkeys have larger ears than horses. Their longer ears may pick up more distant sounds, and may help cool the donkey's blood. Donkeys in the wild can defend themselves with a powerful kick of their hind legs as well as by biting and striking with their front hooves.

Breeding

A 3 week old donkey

Jennies are normally pregnant for about 12 months, though the gestation period varies from 11 to almost 14 months. Jennies usually give birth to a single foal. Twins are very rare: only about 1.7 percent of donkey pregnancies result in twins, and both twins survive in only about 14 percent of cases.

Nutrition

Poitou donkeys.

Donkeys' tough digestive system is somewhat less prone to colic than that of horses, can break down near-inedible vegetation and extract moisture from food very efficiently. As a rule, donkeys need smaller amounts of feed than horses of comparable height and weight. Because they are easy keepers, if overfed, donkeys are also quite susceptible to laminitis.

Woolly paramo donkey

Donkeys evolved to spend 14–16 hours per day browsing and foraging for food. In their native arid and semi-arid climates this would often be a poor quality, scrubby fiber. Domesticated donkey owners face the challenge of feeding their donkey enough low energy fiber in order to meet their appetite, but in temperate climates the forage available is often too rich and abundant, resulting in weight gain and obesity with further implications including laminitis, hyperlipidemia and gastric ulcers. Although the donkey's gastrointestinal tract has no marked differences in structure to that of the horse, it is well documented that "donkeys are more efficient at digesting food than horses and, as a consequence, can thrive on less forage than a similar sized pony". Donkeys need to eat approximately 1.5 percent of their body weight per day in dry matter, compared with 2-2.5 percent for horses. It is not fully understood why donkeys are such efficient digestors but it is thought that they may have a different microbial population in the large intestine than do horses. Another possibility is increased gut retention time compared to ponies.

Donkeys gain most of their daily energy needs from structural carbohydrates. An average, healthy donkey only requires free choice feeding of low-calorie fiber-rich forage such as straw (preferably barley straw), supplemented with controlled grazing in the summer and hay in the winter. A donkey's requirement for protein and fat are so low that in practice once the energy requirements are met so too are the protein and fat requirements. Cereal based feeds designed for horses are often too high in energy levels and will exceed the daily requirements of donkeys. Even a small amount of grazing or fresh fodder during the spring and summer will provide adequate vitamin levels, so for a normal, healthy donkey a diet of straw plus a little grazing or hay meets their nutritional needs without need for concentrated feeds. A low-calorie vitamin and mineral supplement is recommended for donkeys year-round when on a restricted diet, and to all donkeys during the winter months.

Behaviour

Donkeys have a notorious reputation for stubbornness, but this has been attributed to a much stronger sense of "self preservation" than exhibited by horses. Likely based on a stronger prey instinct and a weaker connection with man, it is considerably more difficult to force or frighten a donkey into doing something it perceives to be dangerous for whatever reason. Once a person has earned their confidence they can be willing and companionable partners and very dependable in work.

Although formal studies of their behaviour and cognition are rather limited, donkeys appear to be quite intelligent, cautious, friendly, playful, and eager to learn.

Communication

Satirical use of braying in a political cartoon

Braying is the characteristic sound made by an ass, donkey, and most mules. Donkeys use this sound to communicate and will bray more frequently when a new donkey is encountered. The sound typically lasts for twenty seconds. The sound may be rendered onomatapoeically as "*eeyore*" and so this was used as the name of the donkey in Winnie-the-Pooh. Donkeys may be trained to bray or not to bray upon command. This may be used as a form of mockery. Braying may be considered a simile for loud and foolish speech. For example,

There are braying men in the world as well as braying asses; for what's loud and senseless talking and swearing, any other than braying
—Sir Roger L'Estrange

History

Ancient Greek rhyton in the shape of a donkey's head, ca. 440 BC–430 BC, from Athens. Louvre Museum, Paris.

The ancestors of the modern donkey are the Nubian and Somalian subspecies of African wild ass. The African Wild Ass was domesticated around 4000 BC. The donkey became an important pack animal for people living in the Egyptian and Nubian regions as they can easily carry 20% to 30% of their own body weight and can also be used as a farming and dairy animal. By 1800 BC, the ass had reached the Middle East, where the trading city of Damascus was referred to as the "City of Asses" in cuneiform texts. Syria produced at least three breeds of donkeys, including a saddle breed with a graceful, easy gait. These were favored by women.

For the Greeks, the donkey was associated with Dionysus, the god of wine. The Romans also valued the ass and would use it as a sacrificial animal

Equines had become extinct in the Western Hemisphere at the end of the last Ice Age. However, horses and donkeys were brought back to the Americas by the Conquistadors. In 1495, the ass first appeared in the New World when Christopher Columbus brought four jacks and two jennys. It is from this bloodline that many of the mules which the Conquistadors used while they explored the Americas were produced. Shortly after the United States became independent, President George Washington imported the first mammoth jack stock into the country. Because the existing Jack donkeys in the New World at the time lacked the size and strength he sought to produce quality work mules, he imported donkeys from Spain and France, some standing over 1.63 m tall. One of the donkeys Washington received from the Marquis de Lafayette, named "Knight of Malta", stood 1.43 m and thus was regarded as a great disappointment. Viewing this donkey as unfit for producing mules, Washington instead bred Knight of Malta to his jennys and, in doing so, created an American line of Mammoth Jacks (a breed name that includes both males and females).

Despite these early appearances of donkeys in America, the donkey did not find widespread distribution in America until it was found useful as a pack animal by miners, particularly the gold prospectors, of the mid-19th century. Miners preferred this animal due to its ability to carry tools, supplies, and ore. Their sociable disposition and adaptation to human companionship allowed many miners to lead their donkeys without ropes. They simply followed behind their owner. As mining became less an occupation of the individual prospector and more of an industrial underground operation, the miners' donkeys lost their jobs, and many were simply turned loose into the American deserts. Descendants of these donkeys, now feral, can still be seen roaming the Southwest today.

Ass headcount in 2003

By the early 20th century, donkeys began to be used less as working animals and instead kept as pets in the United States and other wealthier nations, while remaining an important work animal in many poorer regions. The increased popularity of the donkey as a pet in the USA was seen in the appearance of the miniature donkey in 1929. Robert Green imported miniature donkeys to the United States and was a lifetime advocate of the breed and said of it, "Miniature donkeys possess the affectionate nature of a Newfoundland, the resignation of a cow, the durability of a mule, the courage of a tiger, and the intellectual capability only slightly inferior to man's.'

Although the donkey faded from public notice and became viewed as a comical, stubborn beast which was considered "cute" at best, the donkey has recently regained some popularity in North America as a mount, for pulling wagons, and even as a guard animal. Some standard species are ideal for guarding herds of sheep against predators, since most donkeys have a natural wariness toward coyotes and other canines, and will keep them away from the herd.

Donkeys in warfare

Donkeys have been used throughout history for transportation of supplies, pulling wagons, and, in a few cases, as riding animals. During World War I a British stretcher bearer, John Simpson Kirkpatrick, serving with the Australian and New Zealand Army Corps, used a donkey named Duffy to rescue wounded soldiers, carrying them to safety in Gallipoli. There is a statue of John Simpson Kirkpatrick and his donkey in his home town, South Shields.

According to British food writer Matthew Fort, donkeys were, until recently, used in the Italian Army. The Mountain Fusiliers each had a donkey to carry their gear, and in extreme circumstances the animal could be eaten. In 2006, security forces in Afghanistan prevented a man from entering a town in Zabul Province with a donkey which he had laden with 30 kg (66 lbs.) of explosives and a number of landmines, which the man had planned to set off with a remote controlled detonator.

Present status

About 41 million donkeys were reported worldwide in 2006. China has the most with 11 million, followed by Pakistan, Ethiopia and Mexico. Some researchers believe the actual number is somewhat higher since many donkeys go uncounted. The number of breeds and percentage of world population for each of the FAO's world regions was in 2006:

In 1997 the number of donkeys in the world was reported to be continuing to grow, as it had steadily done throughout most of history; factors cited as contributing to this were increasing human population, progress in economic development and social stability in some poorer nations, conversion of forests to farm and range land, rising prices of motor vehicles and fuel, and the popularity of donkeys as pets. More recently, the world population of donkeys is reported to be rapidly shrinking, falling from 43.7 million to 43.5 million between 1995 and 2000, and to only 41 million in 2006.

The Domestic Animal Diversity Information System (DAD-IS) of the FAO listed 189 breeds of ass in June 2011. In 2000 the number of breeds of donkey recorded worldwide was 97, and in 1995 it was 77. The rapid increase is attributed to attention paid to identification and recognition of donkey breeds by the FAO's Animal Genetic Resources project.

In prosperous countries, the welfare of donkeys both at home and abroad has recently become a concern, and a number of sanctuaries for retired and rescued donkeys have been set up. The largest is the Donkey Sanctuary of England, which also supports donkey welfare projects in Egypt, Ethiopia, India, Kenya, and Mexico.

Economic use

On the island of Hydra, because cars are outlawed, donkeys and mules form virtually the sole method of heavy goods transport.

The vast majority of donkeys are used for the same types of work that they have been doing for 6000 years. Their most common role is for transport, whether riding, pack transport, or pulling carts. They may also be used for farm tillage, threshing, raising water, milling, and other jobs. Other donkeys are used to sire mules, as companions for horses, to guard sheep, and as pets. In the past, donkey skin was used in the production of parchment.

A few donkeys are milked or raised for meat; in Italy, which has the highest consumption of equine meat in Europe and where donkey meat is the main ingredient of several regional dishes, only about 1000 donkeys were slaughtered in 2010, yielding approximately 100 tonnes of meat. Asses' milk may command good prices: the average price in Italy in 2009 was €15 per litre, and a price of €6 per 100 ml was reported from Croatia in 2008; it is used for soaps and cosmetics as well as dietary purposes. The niche markets for both milk and meat are expanding.

Donkey cart being loaded in Mapai, Mozambique

Donkeys are often pastured or stabled with horses and ponies, and are thought to have a calming effect on nervous horses. If a donkey is introduced to a mare and foal, the foal will often turn to the donkey for support after it has been weaned from its mother.

Donkeys are now commonly kept as pets in countries where their use as beasts of burden has disappeared. Donkey rides for children are also a popular pastime for children in holiday resorts or other leisure contexts.

Working donkeys may need to be shod. Donkey shoes are similar to horseshoes, but usually smaller and without toe-clips.

Feral donkeys and wild asses

In some areas domestic donkeys have returned to the wild and established feral populations, such as the Burro of North America and the Asinara donkey of Sardinia, Italy, both of which have protected status. Feral donkeys can also cause problems, notably in environments that have been evolutionarily free of any form of equid, such as Hawaii. In Australia, where there may be 5 million feral donkeys, they are regarded as an invasive pest and have a serious impact on the environment. They may compete with livestock and native animals for resources, spread weeds and diseases, foul or damage watering holes and cause erosion.

Wild asses, onagers, and kiangs

With domestication of almost all donkeys few species now exist in the wild. They include the African Wild Ass, *Equus africanus*, and its critically endangered subspecies the Somali Wild Ass, *Equus africanus somaliensis*, and Nubian Wild Ass, *Equus africanus africanus*, the principal ancestor of the domestic donkey. Extinct species include the European Ass, *Equus hydruntinus*, which became extinct during the Neolithic, and the North African Wild Ass, *Equus africanus atlanticus*, which became extinct in Roman times.

There are also five subspecies of Asiatic Wild Ass or Onager, *Equus hemionus*, and three subspecies of the kiang, *Equus kiang*, of the Himalayan upland.

In the wild asses can reach top speeds equalling zebras and even most horses.

Donkey hybrids

A male donkey (jack) can be crossed with a female horse to produce a mule. A male horse can be crossed with a female donkey (jennet or jenny) to produce a hinny. A female donkey in the UK is called a *mare,* or *jenny*.

Horse-donkey hybrids are almost always sterile because horses have 64 chromosomes whereas donkeys have 62, producing offspring with 63 chromosomes. Mules are much more common than hinnies. This is believed to be caused by two factors, the first being proven in cat hybrids, that when the chromosome count of the male is the higher, fertility rates drop (as in the case of stallion x jennet). The lower progesterone production of the jenny may also lead to early embryonic loss. In addition, there are reasons not directly related to reproductive biology. Due to different mating behavior, jacks are often more willing to cover mares than stallions are to breed jennys. Further, mares are usually larger than jennys and thus have more room for the ensuing foal to grow in the womb, resulting in a larger animal at birth. It is commonly believed that mules are more easily handled and also physically stronger than hinnies, making them more desirable for breeders to produce, and it is unquestioned that mules are more common in total number.

The offspring of a zebra-donkey cross is called a zonkey, zebroid, zebrass, or zedonk; *zebra mule* is an older term, but still used in some regions today. The foregoing terms generally refer to hybrids produced by breeding a male zebra to a female donkey. *Zebra hinny, zebret* and *zebrinny* all refer to the cross of a female zebra with a male donkey. Zebrinnies are rarer than zedonkies because female zebras in captivity are most valuable when used to produce full-blooded zebras. There are not enough female zebras breeding in captivity to spare them for hybridizing; there is no such limitation on the number of female donkeys breeding.

Source (edited): "http://en.wikipedia.org/wiki/Donkey"

Eastern Rosella

The **Eastern Rosella** (*Platycercus eximius*) is a rosella native to southeast of the Australian continent and to Tasmania. It has been introduced to New Zealand where feral populations are found in the North Island (notably in the northern half of the island and in the Hutt Valley) and in the hills around Dunedin in the South Island.

Taxonomy

The Eastern Rosella was named by George Shaw in 1792. It is sometimes considered a subspecies of the Pale-headed Rosella (*P. adscitus*). The term White-cheeked Rosella has been used for a species or superspecies combining the Pale-headed and Eastern forms. Hybrids of the two taxa have been recorded where their ranges meet in northeastern New South Wales and southeastern Queensland.

Three subspecies of Eastern Rosella are recognised:
- *P. e. eximius*, Victoria and southern New South Wales. Black feathers on the back have green margins. Rump is pale green.
- *P. e. elecica*, northeast New South Wales and southeast Queensland. In the male the black feathers on the back have golden-yellow margins, and greenish-yellow in the female. The rump is bluish-green. This subspecies is also called the **Golden-mantled Rosella**, often abbreviated to GMR.
- *P. e. diemenensis*, eastern Tasmania. White cheek patches are larger and the red on the head is darker.

Description

Golden-mantled Rosella (*P. e. elecica*) at Woodland Park Zoo, USA. Feathers on the back of the male are edged with a golden-yellow colour.

The Eastern Rosella is 30 cm (12 in) long. It has a red head and white cheeks. The beak is white and the irises are brown. The upper breast is red and the lower breast is yellow fading to pale green over the abdomen. The feathers of the back and shoulders are black, and have yellowish or greenish margins giving rise to a scalloped appearance that varies slightly between the subspecies and the sexes. The wings and lateral tail feathers are bluish while the tail is dark green. The legs are grey. The female is similar to the male though duller in colouration and have an underwing stripe, which is not present in the adult male. Juveniles are duller than females and have an underwing stripe.

Distribution and habitat

The Eastern Rosella is found in lightly wooded country. It eats grass seeds and fruits. Breeding occurs in spring and early summer and up to seven white eggs are laid in tree hollows.

Breeding

Juvenile *P. e. diemenensis*

Chicks in nest

The breeding season is August to January, with one brood. The nesting site is usually a hollow over 1 m (3 ft) deep in a tree trunk anywhere up to 30 m (100 ft) above the ground. A clutch of generally five or six (although up to nine have been recorded) round, white and slightly shiny eggs, measuring 26 x 22 mm, is laid.

As pets

The Eastern Rosella is sometimes kept as a pet. These birds are desired for their beautifully coloured plumage. They are intelligent creatures, which can be trained to whistle a wide repertoire of tunes and may even learn to speak a few words or phrases. Rosellas can make good companion parrots; however, they require a great deal of attention and many toys to satisfy their need for social interaction and mental stimulation. These birds do not always adapt to life as a family pet and even hand-raised birds may never become fully domesticated. Generally, this species does not tolerate "petting" or "cuddling" and is apt to

Feral

A feral horse (an American mustang) in Wyoming, USA

Soay sheep in St Kilda, Scotland

A **feral** organism is one that has changed from being domesticated to being wild or untamed. In the case of plants it is a movement from cultivated to uncultivated or controlled to volunteer. The introduction of feral animals or plants to their non-native regions, like any introduced species, may disrupt ecosystems and has, in some cases, contributed to extinction of indigenous species. However, returning lost species to their environment can have the opposite effect, bringing damaged ecosystems back into balance. By the same token, feral species may eliminate other "problem" species such as rodents, harmful insects, or aggressive plants.

Definitions

In addition to the meaning of the word *feral* described here, from Latin *fera*, "a wild beast", the word has a second unrelated meaning, from Latin *feralis*, "belonging to the dead", "funeral".

Animals

One of the numerous dictionary definitions of a feral animal states that a **feral** animal is an animal which has escaped from a domestic or captive status and is living more or less as a wild animal. Other definitions realize the shortcomings of the first definition and simply say that a feral animal is an animal which has changed from being domesticated to being wild, natural, or untamed.

Zoologists generally exclude from the 'feral' category animals which were genuinely wild before they escaped from captivity: neither lions escaped from a zoo nor the sea eagles (*Haliaeetus albicilla*) recently re-introduced into the UK are regarded as 'feral'. As far as animals are concerned, this article assumes the 'zoological definition' of feral. Some common examples of animals with feral populations are horses, dogs, goats, cats, and pigs.

The term 'feral' should not be used to describe the naturalization of a wild (i.e. non-domesticated) species. Nor should "feral" be used to describe a population of a species which although descended from a domesticated population has severed itself from dependence on humans and lived independently in the wild for a long period.

Plants

Domesticated plants that revert to wild are usually referred to as escaped, introduced or naturalized rather than feral. However, the adaptive and ecological variables seen in plants that go wild closely resemble those of animals.

Variables

Susceptibility

Certain familiar animals go feral easily and successfully, while others are much less inclined to wander and usually fail promptly outside domestication.

Degree

Some species will detach readily from humans and pursue their own devices, but do not stray far or spread readily. Others depart and are gone, seeking out new territory or range to exploit and displaying active invasiveness.

Persistence

Whether they leave readily and venture far, the ultimate criterion for success is longevity. Persistence depends on their ability to establish themselves and reproduce reliably in the new environment.

Tenure of domestication

Neither the duration nor the intensity with which a species has been domesticated offers a useful correlation with its feral potential.

Examples of feral animals

Feral dogs in Bucharest

The cat returns readily to a feral state if it has not been socialized properly in its young life. (See Feral cats.) These cats,

Source (edited): "http://en.wikipedia.org/wiki/Eastern_Rosella"

especially if left to proliferate, are frequently considered to be pests in both rural and urban areas, and may be blamed for devastating the bird, reptile and mammal populations. A local population of feral cats living in an urban area and using a common food source is sometimes called a feral cat colony. As feral cats multiply quickly, it is difficult to control their populations. Animal shelters attempt to adopt out feral cats, especially kittens, but often are overwhelmed with sheer numbers and euthanasia is used. In rural areas, excessive numbers of feral cats are often shot. More recently, the "Trap-Neuter-Return" method has been used in many locations as an alternate means of managing the feral cat population.

A feral goat in Kielder Forest

The goat is one of the oldest domesticated creatures, yet readily goes feral and does quite well on its own.

The dromedary camel, which has been domesticated for well over 3,000 years, will also readily go feral. A substantial population of feral dromedaries, descended from pack animals that escaped in the 19th and early 20th centuries, thrives in the Australian interior today.

Sheep are close contemporaries and cohorts of goats in the history of domestication, but the domestic sheep is quite vulnerable to predation and injury, and thus rarely if ever is seen in a feral state. However, in places where there are few predators, they get on well, for example in the case of the Soay sheep.

Water buffalo run rampant in Western and Northern Australia. This is the only part of the world where they are legally hunted in their original range. The Australian government encourages the hunting of feral water buffalo because of their large numbers.

Cattle have been domesticated since the neolithic era, but can do well enough on open range for months or even years with little or no supervision. Their ancestors, the Aurochs, were quite fierce, on par with the modern Cape Buffalo. Modern cattle, especially those raised on open range, are generally more docile, but when threatened can display aggression. Cattle, particularly those raised for beef, are often allowed to roam quite freely and have established long term independence in Australia, New Zealand and several Pacific Islands along with small populations of semi-feral animals roaming the southwestern United States and northern Mexico. Such cattle are variously called Mavericks, Scrubbers or Cleanskins. Most free roaming cattle, however untamed, are generally too valuable not to be eventually rounded up and recovered in closely settled regions.

Horses and donkeys, domesticated about 5000 BCE, are feral in open grasslands worldwide (*see* feral horse). In Portugal, feral horses are called Sorraia; in Australia, they are called Brumbies; in the American west, they are called Mustangs. Other isolated feral populations exist, including the Chincoteague Pony and the Banker Horse. They are often referred to as "wild horses," but this is a misnomer. There are truly "wild" horses that have never been tamed, most notably Przewalski's Horse. While the horse was originally indigenous to North America, the wild ancestor died out at the end of the last Ice Age. In both Australia and the Americas, modern "wild" horses descended from domesticated horses brought by European explorers and settlers that escaped, spread, and thrived.

Feral donkeys or burros in Nevada

The pig (hog) has established feral populations worldwide, most notably in Australia, New Zealand, the United States, New Guinea and the Pacific Islands. Pigs were introduced to the Melanesian and Polynesian regions by humans from several thousand to five hundred years ago, and to Australia and the Americas within the past 500 years. While pigs were doubtlessly brought to New Zealand by the original Polynesian settlers, this population had become extinct by the time of European colonization, and all feral pigs in New Zealand today are descendants of European stock. Many European wild boar populations are also partially descended from escaped domestic pigs and are thus technically feral animals within the native range of the ancestral species.

Rock Pigeons were formerly kept for their meat or more commonly as racing animals and have established feral populations in cities worldwide.

Colonies of honey bees often escape into the wild from managed apiaries when they swarm; their behavior, however, is no different from their behavior "in captivity", until and unless they breed with other feral honey bees of a different genetic stock, which may lead them to become more docile or more aggressive (see Africanized bees).

Large colonies of feral parrots are present in various parts of the world, with Rose-ringed Parakeets, Monk Parakeets and Red-masked Parakeets (the latter of which became the subject of the documentary film, The Wild Parrots of Telegraph Hill) being particularly successful outside of their native habitats and adapting well to suburban environments.

Rock doves, also known as pigeons: *feral* animals who nonetheless live in close proximity to humans

A Feral Barbary Dove in Tasmania, Australia. Also known as a Ringneck Dove or Ring Dove (*Streptopelia risoria*)

Ecological impact

A feral population can have a significant impact on an ecosystem by predation on vulnerable plants or animals, or by competition with indigenous species. Feral plants and animals constitute a significant share of invasive species, and can be a threat to endangered species.

Genetic pollution

Animals of domestic origin sometimes can produce fertile hybrids with native, wild animals which leads to genetic pollution (not a clear term itself) in the naturally evolved wild gene pools, many times threatening rare species with extinction. Cases include the mallard duck, wild boar, the rock dove or pigeon, the Red Junglefowl (*Gallus gallus*) (ancestor of all chickens), carp, and more recently salmon. Another example is the dingo, itself an early feral dog, which interbreeds with dogs of other origin. However it is seen as unlikely that this will disrupt the ecosystems in which these dogs live and some regard the importance of this phenomenon as disputable. In some cases like rabbits, genetic pollution seems not to be noticed. There is much debate over the degree to which feral hybridization compromises the purity of a wild species. In the case of the mallard, for example, some claim there are no populations that are completely free of any domestic ancestor.

Economic harm

Feral animals compete with domestic livestock, and may degrade fences, water sources, and vegetation (by overgrazing or introducing seeds of invasive plants). Though hotly disputed, some cite as an example the competition between feral horses and cattle in the western United States. Another example is of goats competing with cattle in Australia, or goats that degrade trees and vegetation in environmentally-stressed regions of Africa. Accidental crossbreeding by feral animals may result in harm to breeding programs of pedigreed animals; their presence may also excite domestic animals and push them to escape. Feral populations can also pass on transmissible infections to domestic herds.

Economic benefits

Many feral animals can sometimes be captured at little cost and thus constitute a significant resource. Throughout most of Polynesia and Melanesia feral pigs constitute the primary sources of animal protein. Prior to the Wild and Free-Roaming Horses and Burros Act of 1971, American mustangs were routinely captured and sold for horsemeat. In Australia feral goats, pigs and dromedaries are harvested for the export for their meat trade. At certain times, animals were sometimes deliberately left to go feral, typically on islands, in order to be later recovered for profit or food use for travelers (particularly sailors) at the end of a few years.

Scientific value

Populations of feral animals present good sources for studies of population dynamics, and especially of ecology and behavior (ethology) in a wild state of species known mainly in a domestic state. Such observations can provide useful information for the stock breeders or other owners of the domesticated *conspecifics* (i.e. animals of the same species).

Genetic diversity

Feral populations sometimes preserve or develop characteristics which do not always exist in the fully domesticated equivalent. Therefore, they contribute to domestic biodiversity and often deserve to be preserved, be it in their feral environment or as domestic animals. For example, feral species that are usually subjects of eradication in Australia or New Zealand are currently the subject of study to determine if there is a need for their preservation.

Cultural or historic value

American Mustangs have been protected since 1971 in part due to their romance and connection to the history of the American West.

Source (edited): "http://en.wikipedia.org/wiki/Feral"

Feral Pigeon

Feral pigeons (*Columba livia*), also called **city doves**, **city pigeons** or **street pigeons**, are derived from domestic pigeons that have returned to the wild. The domestic pigeon was originally bred from the wild Rock Pigeon, which naturally inhabits sea-cliffs and mountains. All three types readily interbreed. Feral pigeons find the ledges of buildings to be a substitute for sea cliffs, and have become adapted to urban life and are abundant in towns and cities throughout much of the world.

Cities famous for pigeons

London's Trafalgar Square.

Many city squares are famous for their large pigeon populations, for example, the Piazza San Marco in Venice, and Trafalgar Square in London. For many years, the pigeons in Trafalgar Square were considered a tourist attraction, with street vendors selling packets of seeds for visitors to feed the pigeons. The feeding of the Trafalgar Square pigeons was controversially banned in 2003 by London mayor Ken Livingstone. However, activist groups such as Save the Trafalgar Square Pigeons flouted the ban, feeding the pigeons from a small part of the square that is under the control of Westminster City Council, not the mayor. The organisation has since come to an agreement to feed the pigeons only once a day, at 7:30 a.m.

Food

Perched in Central Park

Eating seeds

Pigeons breed when the food supply is good—for wild rock doves this might be seasonally so they usually breed once a year. In the wild they are often found in pairs in the breeding season but usually they are gregarious. In the urban environment, because of their year-round food supply, feral pigeons will breed continuously, laying eggs up to six times a year.

Feral pigeons can be seen eating grass seeds and berries in parks and gardens in the spring, but there are plentiful sources throughout the year from scavenging (e.g., dropped fast-food cartons) and they will also take insects and spiders. Further food is also usually available from the disposing of stale bread in parks by restaurants and supermarkets, from tourists buying and distributing birdseed, etc. Pigeons tend to congregate in large, often thick flocks when going for discarded food, and many have been observed flying skilfully around trees, buildings, telephone poles and cables, and even moving traffic just to reach it.

Courtship

In foreplay in Kolkata

As a result of the continuous food supply, pigeon courtship rituals can be observed in urban parks at any time of the year. Males on the ground initially puff up feathers at the nape of the neck to increase their apparent size and thereby impress or attract attention, then they single out a female in the vicinity and approach at a rapid walk while emitting repetitive quiet notes, often bowing and turning as they approach. Initially, females invariably walk away or fly short distances, the males follow them at each stage. Persistence by the male will usually eventually cause the female to tolerate his proximity, at which point he will continue the bowing motion and very often turn full- or half-pirouettes in front of the female. Subsequent mating when observed is very brief with the male flapping his wings to maintain balance on the female. Sometimes the male and female beaks are locked together.

Nesting

Buildings are used for nesting as are cliffs and other natural sites.

Nests are rudimentary as for the wild doves and pigeons. Favourite nesting areas are in damaged property. Mass nesting is common with dozens of birds sharing a building. Loose tiles and broken windows give pigeons access; they are remarkably good at spotting when new access points become available, for example after strong winds cause property damage. Nests and droppings will quickly make a mess of any nesting area. Pigeons are particularly fond of roof spaces, many of which accommodate water tanks, though they frequently seem to fall into the tanks and drown. Any water tank or cistern in a roof space needs to have a secure lid for this reason. The popularity of a nesting area seems little affected if pigeons die or are killed there; corpses are seen among live birds, who seem unconcerned.

Many places where pigeons could land are covered with spikes.

On undamaged property the gutters, window air conditioners (especially empty air conditioner containment boxes), chimney pots and external ledges will be used as nesting sites. Many building owners attempt to limit roosting by using bird control spikes and netting to cover ledges and resting places on the facades of buildings. These probably have little effect on the size of pigeon populations, but can help to reduce the accumulation of droppings on and around an individual building.

Only the larger and more wary Common Wood Pigeon (which often shares the same territory and food supply) will build a tree nest; for some reason it prefers trees close to roads.

Cooing

Wendell Levi in his book *The Pigeon* describes the crowing (cooing) in pigeons as mostly being associated with strutting and fighting in cock (male) birds. Hens (females) will coo, but this is noticeably less guttural than the cock birds. Cooing is also more frequent at mating and nesting time between pairs. Both parents share the incubation of their eggs.

Population control

Feral pigeons often only have small populations within cities. For example, the breeding population of feral pigeons in Sheffield, England, has been estimated at only 12,130 individuals. Despite this, feral pigeons usually reach their highest densities in the central portions of cities, so they are frequently encountered by people, which leads to conflict.

A large pigeon trap/coop/loft at Batman Park, Melbourne. Designed specifically to encourage nesting and allow removal of fertilised eggs to prevent population growth, it is a landmark in its own right.

One of the difficulties of controlling pigeon populations is the common practice of feeding them, as here in New York.

Feral pigeons are often considered a pest or even as vermin, owing to concerns that they spread disease and are much maligned in the media for transmitting bird flu, but it has been shown pigeons do not carry the deadly H5N1 strain. Also concerns of them damaging property, causing pollution with their excrement, and driving out other bird species. Some also consider pigeons an invasive species.

While pest exterminators use poison, hawks and nets have also been employed at ground level to control urban pigeon populations, though this generally achieves only a limited, temporary effect.

Long-term reduction of feral pigeon populations can be achieved by restricting food supply, which in turn involves legislation and litter (garbage) control. Some cities have deliberately established favorable nesting places for pigeons – nesting places that can easily be reached by city workers who regularly remove eggs, thereby limiting their reproductive success.

Peregrine Falcons

Peregrine Falcons which are also originally cliff dwellers have also adapted to the big cities, living on the window ledges of skyscrapers and often feeding exclusively on Rock Pigeons. Some cities actively encourage this through falcon breeding programs. Projects include Unibase Falcon project and the Victorian Peregrine Project.

Larger birds of prey occasionally take advantage of this population as well. In New York City, the abundance of pigeons (and other vermin) has created such a conducive environment for predators that the Red-Tailed Hawk has begun to return in very small numbers, the most famous of which is Pale Male.

Poison

Due to their non-selective nature, most avian poisons have been banned. In the United States market only 4-aminopyridine (Avitrol) and DRC-1339 remained registered by EPA. DRC-1339 is limited to USDA use only while 4-AP is a restricted use pesticide, for use only by licensed applicators.

The use of poisons has been proven to be fairly ineffective, however, as pigeons can breed very quickly — up to six times a year — and their numbers are determined by how much food is available; that is, they breed more often when more food is provided to them. When pigeons are poisoned, surviving birds do not leave the area. On the contrary, they are left with more food per bird than before. This attracts pigeons from outside areas as well as encouraging more breeding, and populations are re-established quickly. An additional problem with poisoning is that it also kills pigeon predators. Due to this, in cities with Peregrine Falcon programs it is typically illegal to poison pigeons.

Reducing food supply

A more effective tactic to reduce the number of feral pigeons is deprivation. Cities around the world have discovered that not feeding their local birds results in a safe population decrease in only a few years. Pigeons, however, will still pick at garbage bags containing discarded food or at leftovers carelessly dropped on the ground. Pigeon feeding is banned in parts of Venice, Italy.

Avian contraceptives

In 1998, in response to conservation groups and the public interest, the National Wildlife Research Center (NWRC), a USDA/APHIS laboratory in Fort Collins, Colorado, started work on nicarbazin, a promising compound for avian contraception. Originally developed for use in resident Canada geese, nicarbazin was introduced for use as a contraceptive for feral pigeons in 2007.

The active ingredient, nicarbazin, interferes with the viability of eggs by binding the ZP-3 sperm receptor site in the egg. This unique contraceptive action is non-hormonal and fully reversible.

Pigeons at an automatic feeder

Registered by the EPA as a pesticide (EPA Reg. No. 80224-1), "OvoControl P", brand of nicarbazin, is increasingly used in urban areas and industrial sites to control pigeon populations. Safe and humane, the new technology is environmentally benign and does not represent a secondary toxicity hazard to raptors or scavengers.

Avian contraception has the support of a range of animal welfare groups including the Humane Society of the United States(HSUS), the American Society for the Prevention of Cruelty to Animals (ASPCA) and People for the Ethical Treatment of Animals (PETA).

USDA continues to develop wildlife contraceptives, including the recently registered Gonadotropin-releasing hormone (GnRH) for deer and Diazacon for birds and small mammals. Further development and registrations of Porcine Zona Pellucida or PZP, another immunocontraceptive targeted for feral horses, is supported by HSUS. The new field of wildlife contraceptives is developing rapidly and promises a bright future for the safe, effective and humane management of animal populations.

Dummy egg nesting

Dummy egg nesting programs have been tested in some cities with mixed results. Nest or coop structures are erected and the eggs are removed and replaced with dummy eggs. The eggs are then disposed of to prevent the pigeons breeding. Such structures are being used in New York City and also the Melbourne city centre by the Melbourne City Council at Batman Park. The loft used in Melbourne is on stilts, with a cage door allowing access from beneath for accessing structure at night when the pigeons are asleep.

Source (edited): "http://en.wikipedia.org/wiki/Feral_Pigeon"

Feral cat

A feral cat.

A **feral cat** is a descendant of a domesticated cat that has returned to the wild. It is distinguished from a stray cat, which is a pet cat that has been lost or abandoned, while feral cats are born in the wild; the offspring of a stray cat can be considered feral if born in the wild.

In many parts of the world, feral cats are descendants of domestic cats that were left behind by travelers. As cats are not native to all is especially true on islands where feral cats have sometimes had a substantial and deleterious effect on the local fauna.

Behavior of "feral" cats

Feral versus stray

A feral cat showing typical aggressive behavior

The term *feral* is sometimes used to refer to an animal that does not appear friendly when approached by humans, but the term can apply to any domesticated animal without human contact. Hissing and growling are self-defense behaviors, which, over time, may change as the animal (whether "feral" or "stray") begins to trust humans that provide food, water, and care.

Feral cats that are born and living outdoors, without any human contact or care, have been shown to be adoptable and can be tamed by humans.

Life span and survival

The lifespan of feral cats is hard to determine accurately, although one study reported a median age of 4.7 years, with a range between 0 to 8.3 years, while another paper referenced a mean life span of 2 – 8 years. For contrast, in captivity, an average life expectancy for male indoor cats at birth is 12 to 14 years, with females usually living a year or two longer.

History

During the Age of Discovery, ships released rabbits onto islands to provide a future food source for other travelers. They eventually multiplied out of control and cats were introduced to keep their numbers, and that of mice and rats, down. The cats tended to favor local species as they were ecologically naive and easier to hunt. Their numbers too increased dramatically and soon they colonised many areas and were seen as pests too.

Historical records date the arrival of feral cats in Australia at around 1824. Despite that, it has been suggested that feral cats have been present in Australia since before European settlement, and may have arrived with Dutch shipwrecks in the 17th century, or even before that, arriving from present-day Indonesia with Macassan fisherman and trepangers who frequented Australia's shores.

Diet and predators

Feral cats in Australia prey on a variety of wildlife. In arid and semi-arid environments, they eat mostly introduced European rabbits and house mice; in forests and urbanised areas, they eat mostly native marsupial prey (based on 22 studies summarised in Dickman 1996). In arid environments where rabbits do not occur, native rodents are taken. Birds and reptiles form a smaller part of the diet.

Feral cats may be apex predators in some local ecosystems. In others, they may be preyed on by feral dogs, coyotes, wolves, bears, cougars, bobcats, lynx, fishers, crocodilians, snakes, foxes and birds of prey.

Effects on wildlife

Feral cats can be effective hunters of small animals

The impact of domestic cats on wildlife is a century old debate. In a 1916 report for the Massachusetts State Board of Agriculture titled *The Domestic Cat: Bird Killer, Mouser and Destroyer of Wildlife*, noted ornithologist Edward Howe Forbush stated in the preface: Questions regarding the value or inutility of the domestic cat, and problems connected with limiting its more or less unwelcome outdoor activities, are causing much dissension. The discussion has reached an acute stage. Medical men, game protectors and bird lovers call on legislators to enact restrictive laws. Then ardent cat lovers rouse themselves for combat. In the excitement of partisanship many loose and ill-considered statements are made.

The report referred to *Extinct Birds*, published in 1905 by zoologist Walter Rothschild, who stated, "man and his satellites, cats, rats, dogs, and pigs are the worst and in fact the only important agents of destruction of the native avifaunas wherever they go." Rothschild gave several examples of cats causing the extermination of some bird species on islands.

Feral cats are seen as vermin to many farmers and gamekeepers. The feral cats will catch and eat the ground nesting birds eg: pheasants and partrige. Gamekeepers often set traps and shoot the feral cats as part of pest control on their estate as a way of protecting their birds.

Australia

Feral cat killing a native Australian Cockatoo

Feral cats in Australia have caused the decline and extinction of animals on islands as they have been shown to cause a significant impact on ground birds and small native mammals. Feral cats have also stopped any attempts to re-introduce threatened species back into areas where they have become extinct as the cats have simply hunted and killed the newly released animals. Numerous Australian environmentalists claim the feral cat has been an ecological disaster in Australia, inhabiting most ecosystems except dense rainforest, and being implicated in the extinction of several marsupial and placental mammal species. Although a researcher disagrees with this view (Abbot 2002). Some others believe that there is little sound evidence that feral cats significantly affect native wildlife throughout the mainland and that it is only on the islands that they are a threat (Jones 1989; Wilson et al. 1992). Difficulties in separating the effects of cats from that of foxes (also introduced) and environmental effects have hindered research into this. Cats have co-existed with all mammal species in Tasmania for nearly 200 years. The Western Shield program in Western Australia, involving broad-scale poisoning of foxes, has resulted in rapid recoveries of many species of native mammals in spite of the presence of feral cats throughout the baited area. In 2005, however, a study was published which for the first time found proof of feral cats causing declines in native mammals. An experiment conducted in Heirisson Prong (Western Australia) compared small mammal populations in areas cleared of both foxes and cats, of foxes only, and a control plot. Researchers found mammal populations were lower in areas cleared of foxes only and in the control plots.

Cats may also play a further role in Australia's human altered ecosystems; with foxes they may be controlling introduced rabbits, particularly in arid areas, which themselves cause ecological damage. Cats are believed to have been a factor in the extinction of the only mainland bird species to be lost since European settlement, the paradise parrot.

Australian folklore holds that some feral cats in Australia have grown so large as to cause inexperienced observers to claim sightings of other species such as puma etc. This folklore is being shown to be more fact than fiction, with the recent shooting of an enormous feline, in the Gippsland area of Victoria. Subsequent DNA test showed the feline to be *Felis silvestris catus*. Subsequent news of large feral cat sightings appear almost monthly in Australia, and the evidence is very good to suggest a breeding population of these enormous felines in the southeastern states Victoria and New South Wales.

New Zealand

The fauna of New Zealand has evolved in isolation for millions of years without the presence of mammals (apart from a few bat species). Consequently, birds dominated the niches occupied by mammals and many became flightless. The introduction of mammals after settlement by Māori from about the 12th century had a huge effect on the indigenous biodiversity. European explorers and settlers brought cats on their ships and the presence of feral cats were recorded from the latter decades of the 19th century. It is estimated that feral cats have been responsible for the extinction of six endemic bird species and over 70 localised subspecies as well as depleting bird and lizard species.

Islands

Consequences of introduction

The Stephens Island Wren became extinct within two years of the introduction of cats to Stephens Island

Many islands host ecologically naive animal species; that is, animals that do not have predator responses for dealing with predators such as cats. Feral cats introduced to such islands have had a devastating impact on these islands' biodiversity. They have been implicated in the extinction of several species and local extinctions, such as the hutias from the Caribbean, the Guadalupe storm-petrel from Pacific Mexico, the Stephens Island wren; in a statistical study, they were a significant cause for the extinction of 40% of the species studied. Moors and Atkinson wrote, in 1984, "No other alien predator has had such a universally damaging effect."

Feral cats, along with rabbits, some sea birds, and sheep, form the entire large animal population of the remote Kerguelen Islands in the southern Indian Ocean.

Restoration

Because of the damage cats cause in islands and some ecosystems, many conservationists working in the field of island restoration have worked to remove feral cats. (Island restoration involves the removal of introduced species and reintroducing native species). As of 2004, 48 islands have had their feral cat populations removed, including New Zealand's network of offshore island bird reserves, and Australia's Macquarie Island. Larger projects have also been undertaken, including their complete removal from Ascension Island. The cats, introduced in the 19th century, caused a collapse in populations of nesting seabirds. The project to remove them from the island began in 2002, and the island was cleared of cats by 2004. Since then, seven species of seabird that had not nested on the island for 100 years have returned.

In some cases, the removal of cats had unintended consequences. An example is Macquarie Island (off the coast of Tasmania), where the removal of cats caused an explosion in the number of rabbits, rats, and mice that harm native seabirds. The removal of the rats and rabbits was scheduled for 2007 and it could take up to seven years and cost $24 million.

Hybridisation with wild felids

Feral cats have interbred with wildcats to various extents throughout the world, the first reported case occurring more than 200 years ago. The significance of hybridisation is disputed and hinges on whether the domestic cat is classified as conspecific with the wildcat or a separate species.(see Genetic pollution) In some locations, high levels of hybridisation has led to difficulties in distinguishing a "true" wildcat from feral domestic and domestic hybrid cats, which can complicate conservation efforts. Some researchers argue that "pure" wildcats do not exist anymore, but this is disputed by others. One study in Scotland suggests that while "true" Scottish wildcats are unlikely to exist, the current wildcat population is distinct enough from domestic cats to be worth protecting.

Zoonotic risk

There is concern about the role of feral cat colonies, wild dogs, and other native mammals, as a vector of diseases, particularly toxoplasmosis, giardiasis (esp. from beavers), rabies (e.g. raccoons), *Campylobacter*, Parvovirus and other diseases and parasites that can infect both humans and animals. Felids such as cougars and cats, the mammals they feed on, and undercooked meat and chicken are a source of *Toxoplasma gondii*, which causes toxoplasmosis.

Colonies

Population

Feral cat

A **feral cat colony** (or "clowder") is a population of feral cats. The term is used primarily when a noticeable population of feral cats live together in a specific location and use a common food source. The term is not typically applied to solitary cats passing through an area. A clowder can range from 3-25 cats. Their locations vary, some hiding in alleyways or in large parks.

Members consist of adult females, their young, and some adult males. Unneutered males in a clowder fight each other for territory and for females. Some will be driven out to find another place to live.

Feral cats who have been trapped in many warm areas where fleas exist are usually found to have a large number of fleas, causing them to be anemic. Both the fleas, and the food source, if limited to garbage and rodents, cause the cats to have intestinal microorganisms (such as coccidia or giardia) and other parasites (commonly known as roundworms, tapeworms, and hookworms), which lead to diarrhea and subsequent dehydration. They also can have ear mites, ringworm, and upper respiratory infections. Others are wounded in mating-fights and die from the infected wounds. Still others eventually contract feline immunodeficiency virus or feline leukemia due to the constant transmission of blood and bodily fluids via fighting and sexual activity.

While all of these illnesses are quite treatable, there must be humans to intervene to stop these illnesses from becoming fatal. Due to the number of health problems to which they are subjected, and their fragile immune systems, kittens in the clowders usually do not survive.

A clowder of feral cats

In Trap-Neuter-Return (TNR), volunteers trap feral cats, sterilize them through spaying or neutering, and then release them, though some do keep kittens or cats which are more tame. Variations of the program include testing and inoculation against rabies and other viruses and sometimes long-lasting flea treatments. TNR programs are only now being introduced in some urban and suburban areas, such as Adelaide. More recently, such programs have been introduced in Sydney by the "World League for Protection of Animals". While various long-term studies have shown TNR is effective in stopping the breeding of cats in the wild and reducing the population over time, opponents of TNR frequently cite a study by Castillo (2003) as evidence TNR does not work. Many humane societies and animal rescue groups of varying sizes throughout the United States have some type of TNR program. The practice is endorsed by the Humane Society of the United States and the National Animal Control Association. While the United States Department of Defense does not formally advocate TNR, it does provide information to military installations on how to implement TNR programs. The main message from the department is that population control programs must be humane.

On islands, on which the vacuum effect does not apply, eradication methods include hunting, trapping, poison baiting and biological controls. For example on Marion Island cats were infected with the feline panleukopenia virus, which drastically reduced their population within six years. The remaining cats were killed by shooting.

Feral cats can also be controlled by larger native predators like coyotes, dingoes, or foxes because cats are too small to defend themselves against larger predators.

The multiple, managed, feral colonies at the Colosseum in Rome exceed 250 cats. Other notable colonies include the Canadian Parliamentary Cats, and the cats of Jerusalem

Source (edited): "http://en.wikipedia.org/wiki/Feral_cat"

Feral chicken

A family of feral chickens, Key West, Florida

Feral chickens are derived from domestic chickens (*Gallus gallus domesticus*) that have returned to the wild. Like the Red Junglefowl (the ancestor of domestic chickens), feral chickens will take flight and roost in tall trees and bushes in order to avoid predators at night.

Feral chickens, like the wild Red Junglefowl, typically form social groups composed of a dominant cockerel, several hens and subordinate cocks.

Locations famous for feral chickens

- Bermuda
- Fair Oaks, California
- Galston Gorge, Australia
- Key West, Florida
- Kauai, Hawaii
- Los Angeles, California
- San Juan Bautista, California
- Houston, Texas
- Chicken Roundabout (A143) Bungay, Suffolk, UK
- Port Chalmers, New Zealand
- Totton, UK

Source (edited): "http://en.wikipedia.org/wiki/Feral_chicken"

Feral horse

Feral horse in the Pentland Hills, Scotland

Feral Chincoteague ponies on Assateague Island, Virginia

Feral horses of the Namib

Feral horses in Tule Valley, Utah

Feral horses in Erlebnispark Tripsdrill, near Cleebronn

A **feral horse** is a free-roaming horse of domesticated ancestry. As such, a feral horse is not a wild animal in the sense of an animal without domesticated ancestors. However, some populations of feral horses are managed as wildlife, and these horses often are popularly called "wild" horses. Feral horses are descended from domestic horses that strayed, escaped, or were deliberately released into the wild and remained to survive and reproduce there. Away from humans, over time, these animals' patterns of behavior revert to behavior more closely resembling that of wild horses. Some horses that live in a feral condition but may be occasionally handled or managed by humans, particularly if privately owned, are referred to as "semi-feral."

Feral horses live in groups called a *band*, *herd*, *harem*, or *mob*. Feral horse herds, like those of wild horses, are usually made up of small bands led by a dominant mare, containing additional mares, their foals, and immature horses of both sexes. There is usually one herd stallion, though occasionally a few less-dominant males may remain with the group. Horse "herds" in the wild are best described as groups of several small bands who share a common territory. Bands are usually on the small side, as few as three to five animals, but sometimes over a dozen. The makeup of bands shifts over time as young animals are driven out of the band they were born into and join other bands, or as young stallions challenge older males for dominance. However, in a given closed ecosystem such as the isolated refuges in which most feral horses live today, to maintain genetic diversity the minimum size for a sustainable free-roaming horse or burro population is 150-200 animals.

Feral horse populations

Horses which live in an untamed state but have ancestors who have been domesticated are not true "wild" horses; they are feral horses. The best known examples of feral horses are the "wild" horses of the American west. When Europeans reintroduced the horse to the Americas, beginning with the arrival of the Conquistadors in the 15th century, some horses escaped and formed feral herds known today as Mustangs.

Australia has the largest population of feral horses in the world, with an excess of 400,000 feral horses. The Australian name equivalent to the 'Mustang' is the Brumby, feral descendants of horses brought to Australia by English settlers.

In Portugal, the free-ranging feral horse is known as Sorraia. There are also isolated populations of feral horses in a number of other places, including Sable Island off the coast of Nova Scotia, Assateague Island off the coast of Virginia and Maryland, and Vieques island off the coast of Puerto Rico. Some of these horses are said to be the descendants of horses who managed to swim to land when they were shipwrecked. Others may have been deliberately brought to various islands by settlers and either left to reproduce freely, or abandoned when assorted human settlements failed.

A modern feral horse population (*Janghali ghura*) is found in the Dibru-Saikhowa National Park and Biosphere reserve of Assam, in northern India, a herd of approximately 79 Feral horses descended from animals that escaped army camps during World War II.

Modern feral horses

Modern types of feral horses that have a significant percentage of their number living in a feral state, even though there may be some domesticated representatives, include the following types, landraces, and breeds:

- Banker horse, on the Outer Banks of North Carolina
- Brumby, the feral horse of Australia
- Chincoteague Pony, on Assateague Island off the coasts of Virginia and Maryland
- Cumberland Island Horse, on Cumberland Island off the coast of southern Georgia
- Danube Delta horse, in and around Letea Forest, between the Sulina and Chilia branches of Danube
- ?Elegesi Qiyus Wild Horse (Cayuse), Canada; lives in the Nemaiah Valley, British Columbia
- Kaimanawa horse, New Zealand
- Konduto horse, in the Konduto region, Ethiopia; threatened with extinction
- Misaki Pony, Japan
- Mustang, legally protected by the Wild and Free-Roaming Horses and Burros Act of 1971 in the western United States
- Namib desert horse, Namibia
- Nokota horse
- Sorraia, a feral horse native to Portugal and Spain
- Sable Island Pony found in Nova Scotia
- Welsh Pony, mostly domesticated, but a feral population of about 180 animals roams the Carneddau hills of North Wales. Other populations roam the eastern parts of the Brecon Beacons National Park.

Semi-feral horses

In the United Kingdom, herds of free-roaming ponies live in apparently wild conditions in various areas, notably Dartmoor, Exmoor, and the New Forest. Similar horse and pony populations exist elsewhere on the European continent. These animals, however, are not truly feral, as all of them are privately owned, and roam out on the moors and forests under common grazing rights belonging to their owners. A proportion of them are halter-broken, and a smaller proportion broken to ride but simply turned out for a while for any of a number of reasons (for example a break in training to allow them to grow on, a break from working to allow them to breed under natural conditions, or retirement). In other cases, the animals

may be government-owned and closely managed on controlled reserves.
- Camargue horse, in marshes of the Rhone delta, southern France
- Dartmoor pony, England; predominantly domesticated, also lives in semi-feral herds
- Exmoor pony, England; predominantly domesticated, also lives in semi-feral herds
- New Forest pony, predominantly domesticated, also lives in semi-feral herds in the area of Hampshire, England
- Konik, semi-feral horse of eastern Europe.
- Delft pony, feral herds first introduced by the Portuguese during colonial times to Delft island north of Sri Lanka

Population impacts

Feral populations are usually controversial, with livestock producers often at odds with horse aficionados and other animal welfare advocates. Different habitats are impacted in different ways by feral horses Where feral horses had wild ancestors indigenous to a region, a controlled population may have minimal environmental impact, particularly when their primary territory is one where they do not compete with domesticated livestock to any significant degree. However, in areas where they are an introduced species, such as Australia, or if population is allowed to exceed available range, there can be significant impacts on soil, vegetation and animals that are native species. If a feral population lives close to civilization, their behavior can lead them to damage human-built livestock fencing and related structures. In some cases, where feral horses compete with domestic livestock, particularly on public lands where multiple uses are permitted, such as in the Western United States, there is considerable controversy over which species is responsible for degradation of rangeland, with commercial interests often advocating for the removal of feral horse population to allow more grazing for cattle or sheep, and advocates for feral horses recommending reduction in the numbers of domestic livestock allowed to graze on public lands.

There are certain populations that have considerable historic or sentimental value, such as the Chincoteague pony that lives on Assateague Island, a national seashore with a delicate coastal ecosystem, or the Misaki pony of Japan that lives on a small refuge within the municipal boundaries Kushima. These populations manage to thrive with careful management that includes using the animals to promote tourism to support the local economy. Most sustained feral populations are managed by various forms of culling, which, depending on the nation and other local conditions, may include capturing excess animals for adoption or sale, or the often-controversial practice of simply shooting them. Fertility control is also sometimes used, though it is expensive and has to be repeated on a regular basis.

Source (edited): "http://en.wikipedia.org/wiki/Feral_horse"

Feral parrots

A feral Ringnecked Parakeet on a birdfeeder, Bromley, Kent.

Feral parrot is a term for any parrot that has adapted to life in an ecosystem to which it is not native.

Parrots living in non-native environments

Rainbow Lorikeet

Feral colonies of Rainbow Lorikeet (*Trichoglossus haematodus*) have been established in Perth, Western Australia and in Auckland, New Zealand.

Eastern Rosella

The Eastern Rosella (*Platycercus eximius*) has become naturalized in the North Island of New Zealand.

The population of Red-masked Parakeets that have gone feral in San Francisco have become famous through a book and film that have been made about them.

Rose-ringed Parakeet

A sizeable population of naturalized Rose-ringed Parakeets (*Psittacula krameri*) exists in and around cities in England, the Netherlands, Belgium and western and southern Germany. The largest UK roost of these is thought to be in Esher, Surrey, numbering several thousand. Feral Rose-ringed Parakeets also occur in the United States, South Africa, Israel, Lebanon, UAE and Oman.

Other

Also found in the United States are various naturalized *Brotogeris* spp. (mainly *B. versicolurus* (Canary-winged Parakeet a.k.a. White-winged Parrot) and/

or *B. chiriri* (Yellow-chevroned Parakeet/Parrot).

Brooklyn, New York, in New York City, Austin, Texas and Miami, Florida are home to populations of Myiopsitta monachus (monk aka Quaker Parakeet/Parrot).

A population of naturalized Rose-collared (a.k.a. Peach-faced Lovebirds) (*Agapornis roseicollis*) is found in Tucson, Arizona.

Several species, including Red-lored Parrots (*Amazona autumnalis*), Lilac-crowned Parrots (*Amazona finschi*) and Yellow-chevroned Parakeets (*Brotogeris chiriri*), have become well established in Southern California and a population of mainly Red-masked or Cherry-headed Parakeet/Conure, a female Mitred Parakeet/Conure and thus several inter-specific hybrids live in the area of Telegraph Hill in San Francisco, as depicted in the documentary *The Wild Parrots of Telegraph Hill*.

The Belmont Heights District in Long Beach, California is also known to have many different species of feral parrots which have become local icons to the citizens of the area. They are known for their loud and unique noises as well as their large communities. These parrots can be found roosting mostly on Ocean Boulevard between Livingston Drive and Redondo Avenue in palm trees.

Lists of feral parrot species by continent

North America

Feral Peach-faced Lovebirds eating seeds from a garden feeder in Arizona, USA.

- Budgerigar
- Blue-and-gold Macaw
- Rose-ringed Parakeet
- Monk Parakeet
- Canary-winged Parakeet
- Yellow-chevroned Parakeet
- Peach-faced Lovebird
- Red-lored Amazon
- Lilac-crowned Amazon
- Yellow-chevroned Parakeet
- Red-masked Parakeet
- Hybrid Mitred Parakeet
- Red-crowned Amazon
- Nanday Parakeet

South America

Note: Species found as introduced to the State of Rio de Janeiro, outside their historical ranges; further research can detect other species in other regions.
- Jenday Conure
- Monk Parakeet
- Blue-fronted Amazon

Europe
- Alexandrine Parakeet
- Rose-ringed Parakeet
- Monk Parakeet

Africa
- Rose-ringed Parakeet

Middle East
- Rose-ringed Parakeet

New Zealand
- Rainbow Lorikeet
- Eastern Rosella
- Crimson Rosella

Asia
- Sulphur-crested Cockatoo
- Yellow-crested Cockatoo

Causes

Feral parrot flocks can be formed after mass escapes of newly-imported, wild-caught parrots from airports or quarantine facilities. Large groups of escapees have the protection of a flock and possess the skills to survive and breed in the wild. Some feral parakeets may have descended from escaped zoo birds.

Escaped or released pets rarely contribute to establishing feral populations. Escapes typically involve only one or a few birds at a time, so the birds do not have the protection of a flock and often do not have a mate. Most captive-born birds do not possess the necessary survival skills to find food or avoid predators and often do not survive long without human caretakers. However, in areas where there are existing feral parrot populations, escaped pets may sometimes successfully join these flocks.

The most common era or years that feral parrots were released to non-native environments was during the 1890s to the 1940s, during the wild-caught parrot era.

Controversy

Some bird experts and governments are afraid that the feral parrots may in fact harm the native birds. In fact, parrots are sometimes killed by the government and their species banned from the list of legal pets. They are even listed as the most *dangerous* animals in the state.

However, some people and even some bird experts say that some of these laws should be re-examined. They even keep the non-native European Starling and the Rock Pigeon from making nests. Some governments have let the non-native birds stay in certain places, to avoid problems because a parrot's droppings are wetter than pigeon droppings, which are harder. Some might say, in North America, feral parrots are the replacements to the Carolina Parakeet and the endangered Thick-billed Parrot.

Source (edited): "http://en.wikipedia.org/wiki/Feral_parrots"

Ferret

The **ferret** is a domesticated mammal of the type *Mustela putorius furo*. Ferrets are sexually dimorphic predators with males being substantially larger than females. They typically have brown, black, white, or mixed fur. They have an average length of 20 inches (51 cm) including a 5 inch (13 cm) tail, weigh about 1.5–4 pounds (0.7–2 kg), and have a natural lifespan of 7 to 10 years.

Several other small, elongated carnivorous mammals belonging to the family Mustelidae (weasels) also have the word *ferret* in their common names, including an endangered species, the Black-footed Ferret. The ferret is a very close relative of the polecat, but it is as yet unclear whether it is a domesticated form of the European Polecat, the Steppe Polecat, or some hybrid of the two.

The history of the ferret's domestication is uncertain, like that of most other domestic animals, but it is likely that ferrets have been domesticated for at least 2,500 years. They are still used for hunting rabbits in some parts of the world today, but increasingly they are being kept simply as pets.

Being so closely related to polecats, ferrets are quite easily able to hybridize with them, and this has occasionally resulted in feral colonies of polecat-ferret hybrids that have been perceived to have caused damage to native fauna, perhaps most notably in New Zealand. As a result, some parts of the world have imposed restrictions on the keeping of ferrets.

Biology

Characteristics

As described by the Oakland Zoo, Ferrets have a long and slender body covered with brown, black, white, or mixed fur ... Average length is 20 inches including a 5-inch tail. They weigh 1.5 to 4 pounds, with males substantially larger than females ... Gestation is 42 days, litters are usually 3 to 7 young, but sometimes more. Females may have two to three litters annually. Young are weaned after 3 to 6 weeks and become independent at 3 months. Sexual maturity may come at 6 months. Average life span is 8 years.
—Conservation and Education: Oakland Zoo

Behavior

Ferrets are crepuscular, which means they spend 14–18 hours a day asleep and are most active around the hours of dawn and dusk. Unlike their polecat ancestors, which are solitary animals, most ferrets will live happily in social groups. A group of ferrets is commonly referred to as a "business." They are territorial, like to burrow, and prefer to sleep in an enclosed area.

Like many other carnivores, ferrets have scent glands near their anus, the secretions from which are used in scent marking. It has been reported that ferrets can recognize individuals from these anal gland secretions, as well as the sex of unfamiliar individuals. Ferrets may also use urine marking for sex and individual recognition.

As with skunks, ferrets can release their anal gland secretions when startled or scared, but the smell is much less potent and dissipates rapidly. Most pet ferrets in the US are sold descented (anal glands removed). In many other parts of the world, including the UK and other European countries, de-scenting is considered an unnecessary mutilation.

When excited, they may perform a routine commonly referred to as the weasel war dance, characterized by a frenzied series of sideways hops and bumping into things. Despite its zeal, this is not aggressive but is a joyful invitation to play. It is often accompanied by a soft clucking noise, commonly referred to as dooking. When agitated or upset, on the other hand, ferrets will make a distinct hissing noise.

Diet

Ferrets are obligate carnivores. The natural diet of their wild ancestors consisted of whole small prey, i.e., meat, organs, bones, skin, feathers, and fur.

Dentition

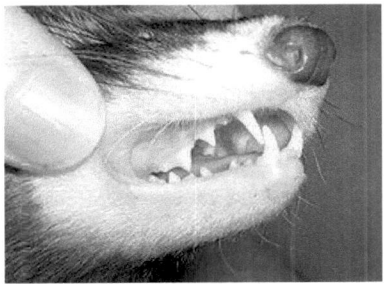

Ferret dentition

Ferrets have four types of teeth (the number includes maxillary (upper) and mandibular (lower) teeth)

- Twelve small teeth (only a couple of millimeters) located between the canines in the front of the mouth. These are known as the incisors and are used for grooming.
- Four canines used for killing prey.
- Twelve premolar teeth that the ferret uses to chew food—located at the sides of the mouth, directly behind the canines. The ferret uses these teeth to cut through flesh, using them in a scissors action to cut the meat into digestible chunks.
- Six molars (two on top and four on the bottom) at the far back of the mouth are used to crush food.

Health

Ferrets are known to suffer from several distinct health problems. Among the most common are cancers affecting the adrenal glands, pancreas, and lymphatic system. Viral diseases include canine distemper and influenza. Health problems can occur in unspayed females when not being used for breeding. Certain health problems have also been linked to ferrets being neutered before reaching sexual maturity. Certain colors of ferret may also carry a genetic defect known as Waardenburg syndrome. Similar to domestic cats, ferrets can also suffer from hairballs and dental problems.

History of domestication

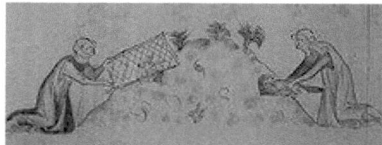

Women hunting rabbits with a ferret in the Queen Mary Psalter

In common with most domestic animals, the original reason for ferrets' being domesticated by human beings is uncertain, but it may have involved hunting. It was most likely domesticated from the European polecat (*Mustela putorius*), although it is also possible that ferrets are descendants of the Steppe polecat (*Mustela eversmannii*), or some hybridization thereof. Analysis of mitochondrial DNA suggests that ferrets were domesticated around 2,500 years ago, although what appear to be ferret remains have been dated to 1500 BC. It has been claimed that the ancient Egyptians were the first to domesticate ferrets, but as no mummified remains of a ferret have yet been found, or any hieroglyph of a ferret, and no polecat now occurs wild in the area, that idea seems unlikely.

The Greek word *ictis* occurs in a play written by Aristophanes, *The Acharnians*, in 425 BC. Whether this was a reference to ferrets, polecats, or the similar Egyptian Mongoose is uncertain. The name "ferret" is derived from the Latin *furittus*, meaning "little thief", a likely reference to the common ferret penchant for secreting away small items. Ferrets were probably used by the Romans for hunting.

Colonies of feral ferrets have established themselves in areas where there is no competition from similarly sized predators, such as in the Shetland Islands and in remote regions in New Zealand. Where ferrets coexist with polecats, hybridization is common. It has been claimed that New Zealand has the world's largest feral population of ferret-polecat hybrids. In 1877, farmers in New Zealand demanded that ferrets be introduced into the country to control the rabbit population, which was also introduced by humans. Five ferrets were imported in 1879, and in 1882–1883, 32 shipments of ferrets were made from London, totaling 1,217 animals. Only 678 landed, and 198 were sent from Melbourne, Australia. On the voyage, the ferrets were mated with the European polecat, creating a number of hybrids that were capable of surviving in the wild. In 1884 and 1886, close to 4,000 ferrets and ferret hybrids, 3,099 weasels and 137 stoats were turned loose. Concern was raised that these animals would eventually prey on indigenous wildlife once rabbit populations dropped, and this is exactly what happened to New Zealand bird species which previously had no mammalian predators.

Ferreting

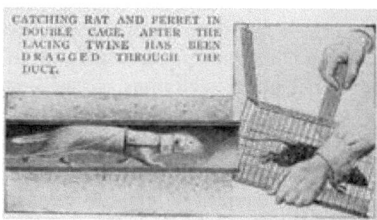

Muzzled ferret flushing a rat, as illustrating in Harding's *Ferret Facts and Fancies* (1915)

For millennia, the main use of ferrets was for hunting, or *ferreting*. With their long, lean build, and inquisitive nature, ferrets are very well equipped for getting down holes and chasing rodents, rabbits and moles out of their burrows, Caesar Augustus sent ferrets or mongooses (named "viverrae" by Plinius) to the Balearic Islands to control the rabbit plagues in 6 BC. They are still used for hunting in some countries, including the United Kingdom, where rabbits are considered a plague species by farmers. The practice is illegal in several countries where it is feared that ferrets could unbalance the ecology. In 2009 in Finland, where ferreting was previously unknown, the city of Helsinki began to use ferrets to restrict the city's rabbit population to a manageable level. Ferreting was chosen because in populated areas it is considered to be safer and less ecologically damaging than shooting the rabbits.

In England, in 1390, a law was enacted restricting the use of ferrets for hunting to the relatively wealthy:

it is ordained that no manner of layman which hath not lands to the value of forty shillings a year shall from henceforth keep any greyhound or other dog to hunt, nor shall he use ferrets, nets, heys, harepipes nor cords, nor other engines for to take or destroy deer, hares, nor conies, nor other gentlemen's game, under pain of twelve months' imprisonment.

Ferrets were first introduced into the New World in the 17th century, and were used extensively from 1860 until the start of World War II to protect grain stores in the American West from rodents.

Ferrets as pets

A ferret in a war dance jump

In the United States, ferrets were relatively rare pets until the 1980s. A government study by the California State Bird and Mammal Conservation Program estimated that by 1996 about 800,000 domestic ferrets were being kept as pets in the United States.

Other uses of ferrets

Ferrets are an important experimental animal model for human influenza, and have been used to study the 2009 H1N1 (swine flu) virus. Smith, Andrews, Laidlaw (1933) inoculated ferrets intranasally with human naso-pharyngeal washes, which produced a form of influenza that spread to other cage mates. The human influenza virus (Influenza type A) was transmitted from an infected ferret to a junior investigator, from whom it was subsequently re-isolated.

- Ferrets have been used in many broad areas of research, such as the study of pathogenesis and treatment in a variety of human disease, these including studies into cardiovascular disease, nutrition, respiratory diseases such as SARS and human influenza, airway physiology, cystic fibrosis and gastrointestinal disease.
- Because they share many anatomical and physiological features with humans, ferrets are extensively used as experimental subjects in biomedical research, in fields such as virology, reproductive physiology, anatomy, endocrinology, and neuroscience.

Terminology and coloring

Typical ferret coloration, known as a sable or polecat-colored ferret

Male ferrets are called hobs; female ferrets are jills. A spayed female is a sprite, a neutered male is a gib, and a vasectomised male is known as a hoblet. Ferrets under one year old are known as kits. A group of ferrets is known as a "business", or historically as a "fesnyng".

Most ferrets are either albinos, with white fur and pink eyes, or display the typical dark masked Sable coloration of their wild polecat ancestors. In recent years fancy breeders have produced a wide variety of colors and patterns. Color refers to the color of the ferret's guard hairs, undercoat, eyes, and nose; pattern refers to the concentration and distribution of color on the body, mask, and nose, as well as white markings on the head or feet when present. Some national organizations, such as the American Ferret Association, have attempted to classify these variations in their showing standards.

There are four basic colors. The Sable (including chocolate and dark), Albino, Dark Eyed White (DEW), and the silver. All the other colors of a ferret are variations on one of these four categories.

Waardenburg-like coloring

Ferrets with a white stripe on their face or a fully white head, primarily blazes, badgers, and pandas, almost certainly carry a congenital defect which shares some similarities to Waardenburg syndrome. This causes, among other things, a cranial deformation in the womb which broadens the skull, white face markings, and also partial or total deafness. It is estimated as many as 75 percent of ferrets with these Waardenburg-like colorings are deaf.

White ferrets were favored in the Middle Ages for the ease in seeing them in thick undergrowth. Leonardo da Vinci's painting *Lady with an Ermine* is likely mislabelled; the animal is probably a ferret, not a stoat, (for which "ermine" is an alternative name for the animal in its white winter coat). Similarly, the Ermine portrait of Queen Elizabeth the First shows her with her pet ferret, which has been decorated with painted-on heraldic ermine spots.

"The Ferreter's Tapestry" is a 15th-century tapestry from Burgundy, France, now part of the Burrell Collection housed in the Glasgow Museum and Art Galleries. It shows a group of peasants hunting rabbits with nets and white ferrets. This image was reproduced in *Renaissance Dress In Italy 1400–1500*, by Jacqueline Herald, Bell & Hyman – ISBN 0-391-02362-4.

Gaston Phoebus' Book Of The Hunt was written in approximately 1389 to explain how to hunt different kinds of animals, including how to use ferrets to hunt rabbits. Illustrations show how multicolored ferrets that were fitted with muzzles were used to chase rabbits out of their warrens and into waiting nets.

Regulation of ferrets as pets

- **Australia** – It is illegal to keep ferrets as pets in Queensland or the Northern Territory; in the ACT a licence is required.
- **Brazil** – They are allowed only if they are given a microchip identification tag and sterilized.
- **New Zealand** – It has been illegal to sell, distribute or breed ferrets in New Zealand since 2002 unless certain conditions are met.
- **Portugal** – It is illegal to keep ferrets as pets in Portugal. Ferrets can be used for hunting purposes only and can be kept only with a government permit.
- **United States** – Ferrets were once banned in many US states, but most of these laws were rescinded in the 1980s and '90s as they became popular pets. Ferrets are still illegal in California under Fish and Game Code Section 2118 and the California Code of Regulations, although it is not illegal for veterinarians in the state to treat ferrets kept as pets. In November 1995, ferret proponents asked the California Fish and Game Commission to remove the domesticated ferret from the restrictive wildlife list. Additionally, "Ferrets are strictly prohibited as pets under Hawaii law because they are potential carriers of the rabies virus"; the territory of Puerto Rico has a similar law. Ferrets are restricted by individual cities, such as Washington, DC, and New York City. They are also prohibited on many military bases. A permit to own a ferret is needed in other areas, including Rhode Island. Illinois and Georgia do not require a permit to merely possess a ferret, but a permit is required to breed ferrets. It was once illegal to own ferrets in Dallas,

Texas, but the current Dallas City Code for Animals includes regulations for the vaccination of ferrets. Pet ferrets are legal in Wisconsin, but an import permit from the state department of agriculture is required to bring one into the state.
- Japan – In Hokkaido prefecture, ferrets must be registered with local government. In other prefectures, no restrictions apply.

Import restrictions
Australia
Ferrets cannot be imported into Australia. A report drafted in August 2000 seems to be the only effort made to date to change the situation.

Canada
Ferrets brought from anywhere except the US require a Permit to Import from the Canadian Food Inspection Agency Animal Health Office. Ferrets from the US require only a vaccination certificate signed by a veterinarian. Ferrets under three months old are not subject to any import restrictions.

European Union
As of July 2004, dogs, cats, and ferrets can travel freely within the European Union under the Pet passport scheme. To cross a border within the EU, ferrets require at minimum an EU PETS passport and an identification microchip (though some countries will accept a tattoo instead). Vaccinations are required; most countries require a rabies vaccine, and some require a distemper vaccine and treatment for ticks and fleas 24 to 48 hours before entry. Ferrets occasionally need to be quarantined before entering the country. PETS travel information is available from any EU veterinarian or on government websites.

United Kingdom
The UK accepts ferrets under the EU's PETS travel scheme. Ferrets must be microchipped, vaccinated against rabies, and documented. They must be treated for ticks and tapeworms 24 to 48 hours before entry. They must also arrive via an authorized route. Ferrets arriving from outside the EU may be subject to a six-month quarantine.

Source (edited): "http://en.wikipedia.org/wiki/Ferret"

Free-ranging urban dog

Three feral dogs from Bucharest, Romania.

Free-ranging urban dog refers to populations of stray dogs on the streets of urban areas, especially the cities of India, the former Soviet Union, and the Balkans.

Stray dogs

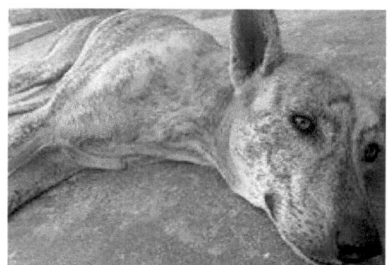

A resting stray in India

Stray dogs are domesticated dogs that lived with people at some point, usually as pets. They have either been abandoned or accidentally released into urban areas, and now fend for themselves. These dogs' offspring are also considered as strays, so the term "stray" may be applied to many generations removed from the original stray founder(s). The World Health Organization also called WHO estimates that there are more than 200 million stray dogs worldwide.

Why do stray dogs exist?
According to the Indian NGO Welfare for Stray Dogs (WSD): "Most free-roaming dogs belong to an ancient canine race known as the pariah dog, which has existed all over Asia and Africa ever since human beings started living in settlements. They are, and have always been, scavengers–that is, they live on garbage created by humans. In India the landrace has existed for perhaps 14,000 years or more. In addition to scavenging, they are widely kept as pets by rural and urban slum households.

Part of the urban stray population consists of mongrels or mix-breeds–descended from pure-breed dogs that have been allowed to interbreed with pariahs.

The size of stray dog populations always corresponds to the size and character of the human population of the area. Urban India has two features which create and sustain stray dog populations:

1) Large amounts of exposed garbage, which provide an abundant source of food.

2) A huge population of slum and street-dwellers, who often keep the dogs as free-roaming pets.

Mumbai has over 12 million human residents, of whom over half are slum-dwellers. At least 500 tons of garbage remain uncollected daily. Therefore, conditions are perfect for supporting a particularly large population of stray dogs."

Problems caused by stray dogs
According to W.S.D: "Haphazard urban planning and human overpopulation have led to a correspondingly huge population of stray dogs in most Indian cities. They cause the following problems:

Rabies can be a fatal disease which can be transmitted to humans. Although all placental mammals can get and transmit rabies, dogs are one the most common carriers. India has the highest number of human rabies deaths in the world (estimated at 35,000 per annum).

Dog bites can occur when dogs are trying to mate or fighting among themselves. Pedestrians and other humans in the vicinity may be bitten by the fighting dogs. Females with pups are often protective and may bite people who approach their litter.

Barking and howling is an accompaniment to dog fights which invariably take place over mating.

Urine smell is an unsavory product of territory marking.

Free-ranging urban dogs in Romania

Stray dog in Romania

In Romania free-ranging urban dogs are usually referred to as: *câinii maidanezi, maidanezii* (ownerless and stray dogs – the strays), *câinii comunitari* (community/communitarian dogs), *câinii vagabonzi* (vagabond dogs), or *câinii străzii* (street-dogs). The online Romanian Explicative Dictionary lists the word *maidanez* as a noun or adjective denoting both ownerless dogs and vagrant, stray dogs (*câine fără stăpân, câine vagabond*). According to the same source, there is also the word *vagabond*, which is a noun or an adjective referring to humans and animals alike. According to estimations in Bucharest, in the year 2000 there were 200,000 free-ranging urban dogs.

Intelligence

Some of the stray dogs in Bucharest are seen crossing the large streets at pedestrian crosswalks. The dogs have probably noticed that when humans cross streets at such markings, cars tend to stop. The dogs have accustomed themselves to the flow of pedestrian and automobile traffic; they sit patiently with the people at the curb when they are stopped for a red light, and then cross with them as if a daily routine.

In culture

Viață de câine (A dog's life) (1998), a Romanian documentary movie by Alexandru Solomon.

Source (edited): "http://en.wikipedia.org/wiki/Free-ranging_urban_dog"

Help Joey

HelpJoey is social initiative launched in 2010 and supported by the ASPCA to raise awareness about overpopulation in companion animals, and the benefits of spaying and neutering.

Purpose

In the United States, over 11,000 pets are euthanized every day. One of the main causes of this overpopulation is owners neglecting to spay and neuter their animals. In an effort to prevent overpopulation Help Joey has made it its mission to go to the source of the problem – the initial conception of a litter – aka – stopping animals from having sex.

Stop Chasing Tail Initiative

To prevent animal overpopulation and animal euthanasia, the movement uses humor to stop animals from having sex, and 'chasing tail.'

Rallying Cry

If animals don't have sex, they can't have babies, therefore no overpopulation problem. So let's just stop animals from having sex?

History of the Movement

Joey Henry, founder of the Help Joey movement, began his effort by heading out into his neighborhood in Tampa, FL finding cats and dogs who were 'doing it' and getting the parties involved to knock it off. After realizing that he could only stop the dogs and cats in his own little world, he rallied his coworker Jesse as a camera man and marketer to film his efforts and start a social movement to gain supporters.

Source (edited): "http://en.wikipedia.org/wiki/Help_Joey"

Indian pariah dog

INDog/Indian pariah dog photographed in a village in Central India, June 2008. The dog belonged to a farmer.

The **Indian pariah dog** is a purebred dog category of pariah dog.

Traits

Pet INDog/Indian Pariah Dog with his owners who belong to the Gond tribe. This picture was taken near Pench Tiger Reserve, Central India.

The aboriginal breed of the Indian subcontinent is called the Indian Pariah Dog, Indian Native Dog and is nowadays referred to as the INDog by experts and enthusiasts. The term "Pariah Dog" is not derogatory in the canine context and refers to a class of primitive dogs of a specific appearance known as the "long-term pariah morph."

From the paper "The Indian Native Dog" by Gautam Das: The Indian Native Dog (INDog) is an ancient autochthonous (landrace) type of dog that is found all over India, Pakistan, Bangladesh and even beyond South Asia. It was featured some years ago on National Geographic Channel's film, 'Search for the First Dog'...along with the other related ancient types such as the Canaan Dog of Israel and the feral Dingo of Australia. This is the original breed of the country, found free-living as a commensal of man all over the Indian subcontinent...Where not mixed with the blood of European dogs or other breeds and types, it is remarkably uniform in appearance all across the entire country...The type represents one of the few remaining examples of mankind's original domestic dog and its physical features are the same as those of the dogs whose fossil remains have been found in various parts of the world, from very early remains in Israel and China to later ones such as those found in the volcanic lava at Pompeii, near Naples in Italy. In India these were the hunting partners and companion animals of the aboriginal peoples of India...they are still found with the aboriginal communities who live in forested areas. Since these dogs have never been selectively bred, their appearance, physical features and mental characteristics are created by the process of natural selection alone. The INDog has not been recognized by any kennel club...even though similarly ancient or 'primitive' dogs have been recognized such as the Azawakh and the Basenji both of which are also sighthound and Pariah. It has been recognized by the Primitive and Aboriginal Dog Society (PADS), a worldwide grouping of enthusiasts which is based in the USA.

Temperament

INDogs are extremely alert and social. They make excellent watch dogs due to their territorial instincts. Their rural evolution, close to forests where predators were common has made them extremely cautious and this caution is not to be mistaken for lack of courage. They bark at the slightest doubt or provocation and hence can be very noisy.

Behaviour

INDogs are found throughout the Indian subcontinent, often kept as pets in remote villages and many are ownerless scavengers found in cities. However the ones in large cities and towns are no longer pure indigenous dogs but are mongrelized with modern breeds.

They are territorial to a particular area, though a certain amount of immigration occurs to maintain population levels and also for the purpose of mating. They are more active and engage in play during mornings and evenings. But during breeding season they become more aggressive during the evening and late night hours to prevent the stranger male dogs and also to protect the pups from other animals including humans. Territorial aggressions are common in free-ranging dogs mostly during breeding season (August to January). On some occasions some males enter into another's territory for extra-group mating.

The pariah group of dogs, including the INDog, breeds once a year. During the mating season the oestrous female may mate with several males. Most of the aggression from the alpha male is directed to the young males, but they are not driven away. When the young males fail in the mating competition, they disperse. As a result the pack size in maintained.

Source (edited): "http://en.wikipedia.org/wiki/Indian_pariah_dog"

Monk Parakeet

The **Monk Parakeet**, also known as the **Quaker Parrot**, (*Myiopsitta monachus*) is a species of parrot, in most treatments the only member of the genus *Myiopsitta*. It originates from the temperate to subtropical areas of Argentina and the surrounding countries in South America. Self-sustaining feral populations occur in many places, mainly in North America and Europe.

Description

Female pet Monk Parakeet

The nominate subspecies of this parakeet is 29 cm long on average, with a 48 cm wingspan, and weighs 100 g. Females tend to be 10-20% smaller but can only be reliably sexed by DNA blood or feather testing. It has bright green upperparts. The forehead and breast are pale grey with darker scalloping and the rest of the underparts are very-light green to yellow. The remiges are dark blue, and the tail is long and tapering. The bill is orange. The call is a loud and throaty *chape(-yee)* or *quak quaki quak-wi quarr*, and screeches *skveet*.

Domestic breeds in colors other than the natural plumage have been produced. These include birds with white, blue, and yellow in place of green. As such coloration provides less camouflage, feral birds are usually of wild-type coloration.

Systematics and taxonomy

Myiopsitta monachus is presently the only unequivocally accepted member of the genus *Myiopsitta*. However, it seems that the Cliff Parakeet (see below) will eventually be recognized as a species again, as it has been on-again-off-again since it was first described in 1868. It is presently included with the Monk Parakeet because there is too little up-to-date research on which an authoritative taxonomic decision could be based. The AOU for example has deferred recognizing the Cliff Parakeet as distinct "because of insufficient published data".

Consequently, there are four subspecies presently recognized:

- *Myiopsitta monachus monachus* (Boddaert, 1783) – Argentina from SE Santiago del Estero Province throughout the Río Salado and lower Paraná basins to Buenos Aires Province and Uruguay

The largest subspecies

- *Myiopsitta monachus calita* (Boddaert, 1783) – Andean foothills up to 1,000 m ASL, from SE Bolivia (Santa Cruz and Tarija departments) to Paraguay and NW Argentina, then west of the range of *monachus*, extending into the lowlands again in Río Negro and possibly Chubut provinces.

Smaller than *monachus*, wings more prominently blue, grey of head darker.

- *Myiopsitta monachus cotorra* (Finsch, 1868) – SW Brazil (Mato Grosso, Mato Grosso do Sul, possibly Rio Grande do Sul) throughout the Río Paraguay and middle Paraná basins as well as the Gran Chaco.

Essentially identical to *calida* but reported as less yellow below and brighter overall.

- **Cliff Parakeet**, *Myiopsitta (monachus) luchsi* (Boddaert, 1783) – Andean valleys of central Bolivia between 1,000/1,300 and 3,000 m ASL, roughly from SE La Paz to N Chuquisaca departments. Essentially the same range as the Red-fronted Macaw.

Smaller, with clearer plumage pattern: no scalloping on breast, underparts brighter yellow, underwing lighter. Base of maxilla dark.

The first three subspecies' ranges meet in the general area of Paraguay, and there they are insufficiently delimited. The distinctness and delimitation of *calita* and *cotorra* especially requires further study. As regards the Cliff Parakeet, it appears as if its altitudinal range does not overlap with that of *calita/cotorra* and that it is thus entirely – but just barely – allopatric.

Like the other Neotropical parrots, the Monk Parakeet is usually placed in the tribe Arini, which might warrant elevation to subfamily rank as Arinae. *M. monachus* belongs to the long-tailed clade of these – macaws and conures, essentially –, which would retain the name Arini/Arinae if this polyphyletic group is split.

Ecology and behavior

Nests in Zaragoza, Spain.

Birds and their nest in Santiago, Chile

The Monk Parakeet is globally very common, and even the rather localized Cliff Parakeet is generally common. In Argentina, Brazil and Uruguay, Monk Parakeets are regarded as major agricultural pests (as noted by Charles Darwin among others). Their population explosion in South American rural areas seems to be associated with the expansion of eucalyptus forestry for paper pulp production, which offers the bird the opportunity to build protected nests in artificial forests where there is small ecological competition from other species. The Cliff Parakeet occasionally plunders maize fields but it is apparently not considered a major pest as there is no serious persecution.

The Monk Parakeet is the only parrot that builds a stick nest, in a tree or on a man-made structure, rather than using a hole in a tree. This gregarious species often breeds colonially, building a single large nest with separate entrances for each pair. In the wild, the colonies can become quite large, with pairs occupying separate "apartments" in nests that can reach the size of a small automobile. These nests can attract many other tenants including birds of prey such as the Spot-winged Falconet (*Spiziapteryx circumcincta*), ducks such as the Speckled Teal (*Anas flavirostris*), and even mammals. Their 5–12 white eggs hatch in about 24 days.

The Cliff Parakeet, as its name implies, rather nests in cliff crevices. This taxon rarely builds communal nests, but individual pairs still prefer to nest in close association.

Unusually for a parrot, Monk Parakeet pairs occasionally have helper individuals, often a grown offspring, which assists with feeding the young (see kin selection).

The lifespan of Monk Parakeets has been given as 15–20 years or as much as 25–30 years; the former might refer to average lifespans in captivity and/or in the wild, while the latter is in the range of maximum lifespans recorded for parakeets.

As pets

Pet with rope and parrot toys

Monk Parakeets are highly intelligent, social birds. Those kept as pets routinely develop large vocabularies. They are able to learn scores of words and phrases.

As an introduced species

Monk Parakeet in San Juan, Puerto Rico

Self-sustaining feral populations have been recorded in several US states and various countries of Europe (namely Spain, Gibraltar and Great Britain), as well as in Brazil, Israel, Bermuda, Bahamas, Puerto Rico and Japan. As it is an open woodlands species, it adapts readily to urban areas.

In areas where they have been introduced, some fear that they will harm crops and native species. Evidence of harm caused by feral colonies is disputed, and many people oppose killing this charismatic bird, but there have been local bans and eradication programs in some areas of the USA. Outside the USA, introduced populations do not appear to raise similar controversy, presumably because of smaller numbers of birds, or because their settlement in urban areas does not pose a threat to agricultural production. Except the UK seems to have changed its view on their feral populations and Defra is to remove Monk Parakeets from the wild. as they believe that the Monk Parakeets threaten local wildlife and crops.

It was found that feral populations are often descended from very small founder populations. Being as social and intelligent as they are, Monk Parakeets will develop some cultural traditions, namely vocal dialects that differ between groups. In populations descended from a large number of birds, a range of "dialects" will exist. If the founder population is small however, a process similar to genetic drift may occur if prominent founders vocalize in an unusual "dialect", with this particular way of vocalizing becoming established in the resulting feral colony. For example, no less than three different "dialects" occur among the feral Monk Parrots of the Milford, Connecticut, metropolitan area.

Brazil

The species has in recent years expanded its range in Brazil, where there is now a self-sustaining population in the downtown area of Rio de Janeiro. Since this population occurs far from the bird's original range in Brazil - it was only found in the far south and southwest - it is most probably a consequence of escapees from the pet trade. In Rio de Janeiro, the bird can be easily seen at the Aterro do Flamengo gardens - where it nests on palm trees and feeds on their fruit; the Rio birds seem to favor nesting amid the leaves of coconut palm trees - as well as in the vicinity of the neighboring domestic flight terminal, the Santos Dumont Airport and in the gardens of Quinta da Boa Vista, where communal nests of roughly one meter in diameter have been seem. In Santa Catarina State, probable escapees have been reported on occasion since quite some time, and a feral population seems to have established itself in Florianópolis in the early 2000s when birds were observed feeding right next to the highway in the Rio Vermelho-Vargem Grande area.

United States of America

Monk Parakeets in Florida, USA.

Considerable numbers of Monk Parakeet were imported to the United States in the late 1960s as pets. Many escaped or were intentionally released, and populations were allowed to proliferate. By the early 1970s, *M. monachus* was established in seven states, and by 1995 it had spread to eight more. There are now thought to be approximately 100,000 in Florida alone.

As one of the few temperate-zone parrots, the Monk Parakeet is more able than most to survive cold climates, and colonies exist as far north as New York City, Chicago, Cincinnati, Louisville, northern New Jersey, coastal Rhode Island and Connecticut, and southwestern Washington. This hardiness makes this species second only to the Rose-ringed Parakeet amongst parrots as a successful introduced species.

In addition, they have also found a home in Brooklyn, New York, after an accidental release decades ago of what appears black-market birds within Green-Wood Cemetery. The grounds crew initially tried to destroy the unsightly nests at the entrance gate, but no longer do so because the presence of the parrots has reduced the number of pigeons nesting within it. The management's decision was based on a comparative chemical analysis of pigeon feces (which destroy brownstone structures) and Monk Parakeet feces (which have no ill effect). Oddly then, the Monk Parakeets are in effect preserving this historic structure. Brooklyn College has a Monk Parakeet as an "unofficial" mascot in reference to the colony of the species that lives in its campus grounds. It is featured on the masthead of the student magazine. Most of these Quaker populations can be traced to shipments of captured Quakers from Argentina.

Due to Quakers' listing as an agricultural pest, California, Georgia, Kansas, Kentucky, Hawaii, New Jersey, Pennsylvania, Tennessee, and Wyoming outlaw sale and ownership of a monk parakeet. In Connecticut, one can own a Quaker, but cannot sell or breed them. In New York and Virginia, it is possible to own a Quaker with banding and registration. In Ohio, owning a Quaker is legal as long as the bird's wings are clipped so that it cannot fly.

Spain

Monk Parakeets in Santa Ponsa, Majorca, Spain.

Monk Parakeets can be seen in Madrid, Barcelona, Cadiz, Valencia, Málaga, Zaragoza, the Canary Islands and Majorca. In Madrid, they especially frequent the Ciudad Universitaria (Complutense university campus) and Casa de Campo park. They are a common sight in Barcelona parks, often as numerous as pigeons. They form substantial colonies in Parc de la Ciutadella, Parc de la Barceloneta, and in smaller city parks such as Jardins Josep Trueta in Poble Nou, with a colony as far north as Empuriabrava.

United Kingdom

The population in 2011 is believed to be around 150 in the Home Counties. The Department for the Environment, Food and Rural Affairs announced plans to control them to counter the threat to infrastructure, crops and native British wildlife by trapping and re-homing, removing nests and shooting when necessary.

Source (edited): "http://en.wikipedia.org/wiki/Monk_Parakeet"

Ossabaw Island Hog

An Ossabaw Hog at the Smithsonian National Zoological Park

The **Ossabaw Island Hog** or **Ossabaw Island pig** is a breed of pig derived from a population of feral pigs on Ossabaw Island, Georgia. The original Ossabaw Hogs are descended from swine released on the island in the 16th century by Spanish explorers. A breeding population has been established on American farms off the island, but they remain a critically endangered variety of pig.

History

As the Spanish explored the coast of the Americas in the 16th century, livestock such as pigs were often left on islands as a future food source. This was the origin of the pigs that would become the Ossabaw breed. Over the following hundreds of years, the population of these feral pigs remained isolated on Ossabaw, which is one of the Sea Islands, barrier islands off the Georgia coast, and there was very little introduction of other domestic breeds. Since 1978 the island has been owned by the State and managed by the Georgia Department of Natural Resources (DNR) as a preserve.

The human population of the island was never high, and the pigs generally ranged freely over its entire acreage. Like feral pigs elsewhere in the world, those on Ossabaw have had an adverse effect on native habitat and species. The pigs are highly omnivorous, and will consume everything from roots and tubers to small reptiles and mammals. Ossabaw Hogs have even been observed feeding on White-tailed deer entrails.

Ossabaw Island Hogs have been documented as having a negative impact on endangered species such as the Loggerhead Sea Turtle and Snowy Plover, disturbing nests and eating eggs. This, plus the varied other impacts they have on the ecosystem, have convinced the Georgia Department of Natural Resources to recommend the eradication of all feral swine via trapping, shooting and hunting by the public.

Aside from the environmental concerns posed by Ossabaw Island Hogs, they are also recognized as a unique genetic resource by scientists and breed conservationists. They are thought to be the only U.S. breed which is descended from the Iberian-type pigs brought to North America by the Spanish. A very small breeding population of Ossabaw Hogs are kept off the island by farmers who market them as a form of heritage pork, and there are also herds at several zoos, at Mount Vernon and at Colonial Williamsburg. Captive breeding populations were also previously kept by a few American universities for scientific study and conservation, but these herds were dissolved and have not contributed to the current bloodlines of Ossabaw Hogs on the mainland today.

Both the island and mainland populations continue to be considered vulnerable by the ALBC, Slow Food, and others. The breed is listed as "critical" on the priority list of the American Livestock Breeds Conservancy, and is also included in Slow Food USA's Ark of Taste, a catalog of heritage foods in danger of extinction.

The population on the island is currently controlled by the methods advised by the DNR, and it is unclear how much longer the population will avoid eradication entirely. Due to the presence of porcine vesicular stomatitis and pseudorabies on the island, no more live pigs may be removed from the island. The mainland U.S. population kept by farmers is preserved because of interest from the sustainable agriculture movement.

Characteristics

An Ossabaw Island Hog with a spotted coat

The breed characteristics of Ossabaw Island Hogs in both phenotype and genotype have been shaped by the pressures of feral life in an island habitat. They are small swine, less than 20 inches (510 mm) tall and weighing less than 200 pounds (90 kg) at maturity. This size is partly due to the phenomenon of insular dwarfism, and individuals kept in off-island farms may grow slightly larger in successive generations. They are also hardy and very good foragers, making them useful in extensive farming (as opposed to intensive pig farming).

Ossabaw Hogs appear in a wide range of colors, with the most common being black and a spotted variety. Ossabaw piglets do not show the striping that Wild Boars do, and because of their isolation on the island they are not hybridized, as the Razorback may be. They additionally have long snouts, upright ears, and a heavy coat of bristles compared to other pig breeds. Ossabaws are noted to be intelligent and friendly swine in terms of temperament.

As a result of life on an island where the abundance and scarcity of food is seasonally variable, Ossabaw Hogs store fat in a different manner than most domestic pigs and have a "thrifty gene". In conditions with constant supplies of food (such as on farms and in the laboratory) they accrue more fat than other pigs and may develop a "prediabetes" condition. Because this trait makes them useful as a model organism, scientific studies on metabolic syndrome

Overpopulation in companion animals

The phenomenon of **overpopulation in companion animals** refers to the large number of homeless domestic cats and dogs. In the United States alone, between 3 and 4 million cats and dogs are euthanized each year because no one volunteers to adopt them. As a result, most humane societies, animal shelters and rescue groups urge animal caregivers to have their animals spayed or neutered to prevent the births of unwanted and accidental litters.

Effects upon animals

Unwanted and stray dogs and cats suffer from neglect and abandonment, deplorable living conditions, insufficient or nonexistent veterinary care, and substandard veterinary practices. Such animals are often victimized by people who treat them inhumanely, due to poverty, lack of knowledge of how to provide care, absence of animal welfare legislation and enforcement, apathy, personal beliefs, and intentional cruelty.
Source (edited): "http://en.wikipedia.org/wiki/Overpopulation_in_companion_animals"

Pariah dog

Indian Pariah-type feral dogs are typically medium-sized and have yellow to rust-colored coats.

The term **pariah dog** (also **pye dogs**, or **pi dogs**) originally referred to Chinese/Indian feral dogs of a particular type, but it is now used by the United Kennel Club to refer to a purebred dog category.

Feral dogs of India

Pariah-type feral dogs are typically medium-sized and have yellow to rust-colored coats. It was once thought that Indian feral dogs were the ancestral stock of Australian dingoes, but a 2004 Swedish study of mitochondrial DNA found that dingoes originated from southern China, not from India.

The Sighthound & Pariah Group

The United Kennel Club (United States) recognizes purebred dogs bred for chasing large game in the Sighthound & Pariah Group. Included in this group are breeds that are either of early origin or modern reconstructions of early breeds or types. The group includes the Afghan Hound, Azawakh, Basenji, Borzoi, Canaan Dog, Carolina Dog, Chart Polski (Polish Greyhound), Cirneco dell'Etna, Greyhound, Hungarian Greyhound, Ibizan Hound, Irish Wolfhound, New Guinea Singing Dog, Pharaoh Hound, Portuguese Podengo, Rhodesian Ridgeback, Saluki, Scottish Deerhound, Sloughi, Spanish Greyhound, Thai Ridgeback, Whippet, and Xoloitzcuintli.

In place of "pariah" (pariah is derived from the Tamil word *paraiyar*, first used in English in 1613 to refer to the lowest level of the traditional Indian caste system; in English, it is used to mean "social outcast"), most registries, other than United Kennel Club, use the term "primitive" (primitive in the sense of "relating to an earliest or original stage or state" or "being little evolved from an early ancestral type") to refer to pariah-type dogs. The American Rare Breed Association, for example, places its Pariah-type dogs within a breed group designated "Spitz and Primitive."

Varieties of pariah dogs

Populations of pariah dogs are distributed in India, Thailand, Myanmar, Southeast China, Laos, Malaysia, Thailand, Indonesia, Singapore, Borneo, United States, Korea, and the Philippines.

The Carolina Dog found in the southeastern United States of America is one example of a pariah-type feral dog. The Carolina Dog closely resembles feral dogs found in deserts of middle eastern countries. Both the desert dog (known as the Canaan Dog) and Carolina Dog are recognized as purebred by major registries.

All strains of pariah dogs are at risk of losing their genetic uniqueness by interbreeding with purebred and mixed-breed strays. To insure against this, some strains of pariah dogs are becoming formally recognized, registered, and pedigreed breeds as their fanciers attempt to preserve the pure type.

All pariah dogs are feral, but not all feral dogs are pariah dogs in the genetic sense. Though they are outcasts in the social sense, and thus may still be called pariahs by observers who are not dog fanciers, feral dogs may be of any breed or mix of breeds. The individuals may be stray pets, or descended from strays, or from litters dumped in wild or rural areas by irresponsible owners. They may form packs with other strays or attempt to join existing canid packs (such as a wolf pack). While pariah dogs are by definition feral, pariah-type dogs are not necessarily feral (wild dog populations which have not been re-domesticated), as well as recognized dog breeds with pariah dog heritage.

Readers of a literary but non-canine bent will recognize "a pack of pariah dogs" from Saki (H.H. Munro)'s brief story, "The Open Window".
Source (edited): "http://en.wikipedia.org/wiki/Pariah_dog"

Rabbits in Australia

A European Rabbit in Tasmania.

In Australia, **rabbits** are a serious mammalian pest and are an invasive species. Annually, European rabbits cause millions of dollars of damage to crops.

Effects on Australia's ecology

Erosion of a gully in South Australia caused by rabbits.

Since their introduction from Europe in the 19th century, the effect of rabbits on the ecology of Australia has been devastating. Rabbits are suspected of being the most significant known factor in species loss in Australia. The loss of plant species is unknown at this time. Rabbits often kill young trees in orchards, forests and on properties by ringbarking them.

Rabbits are also responsible for serious erosion problems as they eat native plants, leaving the topsoil exposed and vulnerable to sheet, gully and wind erosion. The removal of this topsoil is devastating to the land as it takes many hundreds of years to regenerate.

Rabbits were first introduced to Australia by the First Fleet in 1788. They were bred as food animals, probably in cages. In the first decades they do not appear to have been numerous, judging from their absence from archaeological collections of early colonial food remains. However, by 1827 in Tasmania a newspaper article noted '…the common rabbit is becoming so numerous throughout the colony, that they are running about on some large estates by thousands. We understand, that there are no rabbits whatever in the elder colony' [i.e. New South Wales]. This clearly shows that a localised rabbit population explosion was underway in Tasmania in the early 19th century. At the same time in NSW Cunningham noted that '... rabbits are bred around houses, but we have yet no wild ones in enclosures...' He noted that the scrubby, sandy soil between Sydney and Botany Bay would be ideal for farming rabbits. Enclosures appears to mean more extensive rabbit-farming warrens, rather than cages. The first of these, in Sydney at least, was one built by Alexander Macleay at Elizabeth Bay House,'a preserve or rabbit-warren, surrounded by a substantial stone wall, and well stocked with that choice game'. In the 1840s rabbit-keeping became even more common, with examples of the theft of rabbits from ordinary peoples' houses appearing in court records, and rabbits entering the diet of ordinary people.

A question remains as to why there was no outbreak before the start of the current infestation. The localised Tasmanian rabbit plague was noted, but it would be surprising if there were no escapes from the many warrens and cages that would have been present throughout the area of European settlement in southeastern Australia. It is possible that native predators, particularly carnivorous dasyurids, were much more effective as natural controllers of the population than the later foxes and feral cats. When their populations collapsed as a result of habitat destruction, and sometimes deliberate hunting, rabbit populations could rise with far less restraint.

The current infestation appears to have originated with the release of 12 wild rabbits by Thomas Austin on his property, *Barwon Park*, near Winchelsea, Victoria, in October 1859 for hunting purposes. While living in England, Austin had been an avid hunter, regularly dedicating his weekends to rabbit shooting. Upon arriving in Australia, which had no native rabbit population, Austin asked his nephew William Austin in England to send him 12 grey rabbits, five hares, 72 partridges and some sparrows so that he could continue his hobby in Australia by creating a local population of the species. However William could not source enough grey rabbits to meet his uncle's order. So he topped it up by buying domestic rabbits. One theory as to why the Barwon park rabbits adapted so well to Australia is that the hybrid rabbits that resulted from the interbreeding of the two distinct types were particularly hardy and vigorous. Many other farms released their rabbits into the wild after Austin. At the time he had stated, "The introduction of a few rabbits could do little harm and might provide a touch of home, in addition to a spot of hunting."

Rabbits are extremely prolific creatures, and spread rapidly across the southern parts of the country. Australia had ideal conditions for a rabbit population explosion. With mild winters, rabbits were able to breed the entire year. With widespread farming, areas that may have been scrub or woodlands were instead turned into vast areas with low vegetations, creating ideal habitat for rabbits.

In a classic example of unintended consequences, within ten years of their introduction in 1859, rabbits had become so prevalent that two million could be shot or trapped annually without having any noticeable effect on the population. It was the fastest spread ever recorded of any mammal anywhere in the world. Today rabbits are entrenched in the southern and central areas of the country, with scattered populations in the northern deserts.

Although the rabbit is a notorious pest it proved helpful to many people during the Great Depression and during wartime. Trapping rabbits helped farmers, stockmen and stationhands by providing something to eat, extra income and in some cases helped pay off farming debts. Rabbits were fed to working dogs, and boiled to be fed to the poultry. Later, frozen rabbit carcases were traded locally and exported. Pelts too, were used in the fur trade and are still used in the felt-hat industry.

Control measures

A load of rabbit skins, Northern Tablelands, New South Wales

An old poison cart which buried poisoned baits to kill rabbits, Woolbrook, NSW

A Royal Commission was held to investigate the situation in 1901. Once the problem was understood, various control methods were tried to limit or reduce the population of rabbits in Australia. These methods had limited success until the introduction of biological control methods in the latter half of the 20th century.

Conventional control measures

Shooting rabbits is one of the most common control methods. However, this has little noticeable effect on rabbit populations.

Destroying warrens through ripping (a procedure where rabbits are dismembered or buried alive as a bulldozer dragging sharp tines is driven over their warrens/burrows), ploughing, blasting, and fumigating is widely used especially on large farms (known as 'stations'). The sandy soil in many parts of Australia makes ripping and ploughing a viable method of control, and both tractors and bulldozers are used for this operation.

Poisoning is probably the most widely-used of the conventional techniques, as it requires the least effort. The disadvantage is that the rabbit cannot be used as food for either humans or pets afterward. Two commonly-used poisons for rabbit control are sodium fluoroacetate ("1080") and pindone.

Another technique is hunting using ferrets, where ferrets are deployed to chase the rabbits out to be shot or into nets set over the burrows. Since ferrets are limited in the number of rabbits they can kill, this is more a hunting activity than a serious control method.

Historically, trapping was also frequently used; steel-jawed leg-holding traps were banned in most states in the 1980s on animal cruelty grounds, though trapping continues at a lower level using rubber-jawed traps. All of these techniques are limited to working only in settled areas and are quite labour-intensive.

In 1907, the rabbit-proof fence was built in Western Australia between Cape Keraudren and Esperance to try to control the rabbit population. European rabbits can both jump very high and burrow underground. Even assuming a perfectly intact fence stretching for hundreds of miles, and assuming that farmers or graziers do not leave gates open for livestock or machinery it was unlikely to be a success.

Biological measures

Rabbits around a waterhole in the myxomatosis trial site on Wardang Island in 1938.

Releasing rabbit-borne diseases has proven somewhat successful in controlling the population of rabbits in Australia. In 1950, after research carried out by Frank Fenner, Myxomatosis was deliberately released into the rabbit population, causing it to drop from an estimated 600 million to around 100 million. Genetic resistance in the remaining rabbits allowed the population to recover to 200-300 million by 1991.

To combat this trend, Commonwealth Scientific and Industrial Research Organisation (CSIRO) developed and accidentally released calicivirus (also known as Rabbit Haemorrhagic Disease or RHD) in 1996. The success of the virus was found to be higher in extreme heat. This was because it appears there is another calicivirus in the colder, wetter areas of Australia, and that this virus was immunising rabbits against the more virulent form.

A legal vaccine exists in Australia for RHD. There is no cure for either Myxomatosis or RHD, and many affected pets are euthanised. In Europe, where rabbits are farmed on a large scale, they are protected against myxomatosis and calicivirus with a genetically modified virus. The vaccine was developed in Spain.

Source (edited): "http://en.wikipedia.org/wiki/Rabbits_in_Australia"

Rainbow Lorikeet

The **Rainbow Lorikeet** (*Trichoglossus haematodus*) is a species of Australasian parrot found in Australia, eastern Indonesia (Maluku and Western New Guinea), Papua New Guinea, New Caledonia, Solomon Islands and Vanuatu. In Australia, it is common along the eastern seaboard, from Queensland to South Australia and northwest Tasmania. Its habitat is rainforest, coastal bush and woodland areas. Several taxa traditionally listed as subspecies of the Rainbow Lorikeet are increasingly treated as separate species (see *Taxonomy*).

Rainbow Lorikeets have been introduced to Perth - Western Australia, Auckland - New Zealand, and Hong Kong. - China

Taxonomy

Rainbow Lorikeets are true parrots, within the Psittacidae family, which are contained in the order Psittaciformes.

The Rainbow Lorikeet has often included the Red-collared Lorikeet (*T. rubritorquis*) as a subspecies, but today most major authorities consider it separate. Additionally, a review in 1997 led to the recommendation of splitting off some of the most distinctive taxa from the Lesser Sundas as separate species, these being the Scarlet-breasted Lorikeet (*T. forsteni*), the Marigold Lorikeet (*T. capistratus*) and the Flores Lorikeet (*T. weberi*). This is increasingly followed by major authorities. With these as separate species, the Rainbow Lorikeet includes the following subspecies (in taxonomic order); most of the common names listed below are only used in aviculture.
- Rosenberg's or Biak Lorikeet, *T. h. rosenbergii* - Biak Island, Indonesia. Very distinctive, and possibly worthy of treatment as a separate species.
- Blue-faced Lorikeet, *T. h. intermedius*. - north coast of New Guinea. Not always considered distinct from *T. h. haematodus*.
- Green-naped Lorikeet, *T. h. haematodus* - southern Maluku, West Papua islands and western New Guinea.
- Dark-throated Lorikeet, *T. h. nigrogularis* - Kai Islands, Aru Islands and southern New Guinea. If *T. h. caeruleiceps* is recognized, *T. h. nigrogularis* is restricted to the Kai and Aru Islands.
- Brook's Lorikeet, *T. h. brooki* - Spriti Island in the Aru Islands. Not always considered distinct from *T. h. nigrogularis*.
- Pale-head Lorikeet, *T. h. caeruleiceps* - southern New Guinea. Not always considered distinct from *T. h. nigrogularis*.
- Southern Green-naped Lorikeet, *T. h. micropteryx* - east New Guinea.
- Ninigo Lorikeet, *T. h. nesophilus* - Ninigo and Hermit Groups, west of Manus Island, Papua New Guinea.
- Olive-green Lorikeet, *T. h. flavicans* - New Hanover Island, St. Matthias Islands and Admiralty Islands.
- Massena's or Coconut Lorikeet, *T. h. massena* - eastern New Guinea, Louisiade Archipelago, Karkar Island, Bismarck Archipelago, Solomon Islands and Vanuatu.
- Deplanche's Lorikeet, *T. h. deplanchii* - New Caledonia and Loyalty Islands.
- Swainson's Lorikeet, *T. h. moluccanus* - eastern Australia and Tasmania. The population of the Cape York Peninsula and the Torres Strait Islands is now often treated as a separate subspecies, *T. h. septentrionalis*.

Images of subspecies

Swainson's Lorikeet
T. h. moluccanus

Rosenberg's Lorikeet
T. h. rosenbergii at Nashville Zoo, USA

Green-naped Lorikeet
T. h. haematodus

Description

The well known subspecies *T. h. moluccanus* has a blue belly and lacks the barring on the breast found on the nominate subspecies

The Rainbow Lorikeet is a medium sized parrot, with the length ranging from 25–30 cm (9.8-11.8 in) in size, and has a wingspan of about 17 cm (6.7 in). The weight varies from 75–157 g (2.6–5.5 oz). The plumage of the nominate race, as with all subspecies, is very bright. The head is deep blue with a greenish-yellow nuchal collar, and the rest of the upperparts (wings, back and tail) are deep green. The chest is red with blue-black barring. The belly is deep green, and the thighs and rump are yellow with deep green barring. In flight a yellow wing-bar contrasts clearly with the red underwing coverts. There is little to visually distinguish between the sexes. Juveniles have a black beak which gradually brightens to orange in the adults. The markings of the best known subspecies *T. h. moluccanus* resemble those of the nominate race, but with a blue belly and a more orange breast with little or no blue-black barring. Other subspecies largely resemble either the nominate race or *T. h. moluccanus*, or are intermediate between them. Two exceptions are *T. h. flavicans* and *T. h. rosenbergii*. In the rather variable *T. h. flavicans* the green of some individuals is dull, almost olivaceous, but in others the green hue approaches that typical of the Rainbow Lorikeet. *T. h. rosenbergii* is highly distinctive and several features separates it from all other subspecies: Its wing-bars are deep orange (not contrasting clearly with the red underwing coverts in flight), the entire nape is yellow bordered by a narrow red band and the dark blue barring to the red chest is very broad.

Behaviour

Rainbow Lorikeets often travel together in pairs and occasionally respond to calls to fly as a flock, then disperse again into pairs. Rainbow Lorikeet pairs defend their feeding and nesting areas aggressively against other Rainbow Lorikeets and other bird species. They chase off not only smaller birds such as the Noisy Miner, but also larger and more powerful birds such as the Australian Magpie.

Diet

In Brisbane, Queensland. The yellow wing-bar is present in all subspecies, except *T. h. rosenbergii* where it is deep orange

Rainbow Lorikeets feed mainly on fruit, pollen and nectar, and possess a tongue adapted especially for their particular diet. The end of the tongue is equipped with a papillate appendage adapted to collecting nectar from flowers. Nectar from eucalyptus are important in Australia, other important nectar sources are *Pittosporum*, *Grevillea*, *Spathodea campanulata* (African Tulip-tree), and sago palm. In Melanesia coconuts are very important food sources, and Rainbow Lorikeets are important pollinators of these. They also consume the fruits of *Ficus*, *Trema*, *Mutingia*, as well as papaya and mangoes already opened by fruit bats. They also eat crops such as apples, and will raid maize and sorghum. They are also frequent visitors at bird feeders placed in gardens, which supply store-bought nectar, sunflower seeds, and fruits such as apples, grapes and pears.

In many places, including campsites and suburban gardens, wild lorikeets are so used to humans that they can be hand-fed. The Currumbin Wildlife Sanctuary in Queensland, Australia, is noted for its numerous lorikeets, which number in the thousands. Around 8am and 4pm each day the birds gather in a huge, noisy flock in the park's main area. Visitors are encouraged to feed them a specially prepared nectar, and the birds will happily settle on arms and heads to consume it. Wild Rainbow Lorikeets can also be hand-fed by visitors at Lone Pine Koala Sanctuary in Brisbane, Queensland, Australia. Semitame lorikeets are common daily visitors in Sydney backyards, often by the dozens.

Rainbow Lorikeets can also be fed in many zoos and animal parks outside Australia.

Breeding

In Australia, breeding usually occurs during spring (September to December), but can vary from region to region with changes in food availability and climate. Nesting sites are variable and can include hollows of tall trees such as eucalypts, palm trunks, or overhanging rock. One population in the Admiralty Islands nests in holes in the ground on predator-free islets. Pairs sometimes nest in the same tree with other Rainbow Lorikeet pairs, or other bird species. The clutch size is between one to three eggs, which are incubated for around 25 days. Incubation duties are carried out by the female alone.

Status

Overall, the Rainbow Lorikeet remains widespread and often common. It is therefore considered to be of Least Concern by BirdLife International. The status for some localised subspecies is more precarious, with especially *T. h. rosenbergii* (which possibly is worthy of treatment as a separate species) being threatened by habitat loss and capture for the parrot trade.

As a pest

Introduced to Western Australia

The Rainbow Lorikeet was accidentally released into the southwest of the state of Western Australia from the University of Western Australia in the 1960s and they have since been classified as a pest.

Rainbow Lorikeets can also be found in New Zealand, particularly around the Auckland area. New Zealand's Department of Conservation has declared them a pest and is implementing methods to control and eradicate them.

Many fruit orchard owners consider them a pest, as they often fly in groups and strip trees containing fresh fruit. In urban areas, the birds create nuisance noise and fouling of outdoor areas and vehicles with droppings.

In Western Australia, a major impact of the Rainbow Lorikeet is competition with indigenous bird species. This includes domination of feeding resources, and competition for increasingly scarce nesting hollows. Birds such as the Purple-crowned Lorikeet *Glossopsitta porphyrocephala* and Carnaby's Black-Cockatoo *Calyptorhynchus latirostris* are adversely affected or displaced.
Source (edited): "http://en.wikipedia.org/wiki/Rainbow_Lorikeet"

Red-crowned Amazon

The **Red-crowned Amazon**, (*Amazona viridigenalis*) also known as **Red-crowned Parrot**, **Green-cheeked Amazon**, or **Mexican Red-headed Parrot**, is an endangered Amazon parrot native to northeastern Mexico. The current native wild population of between 1,000 and 2,000 is decreasing. The main threats to its survival are the illegal export of trapped birds from Mexico to the United States and the destruction of habitat.

Description

Head and neck

Their appearance is generally green with the most notable features being a bright red forehead and crown, dark blue streaks behind the eyes, and light green cheeks.

Range

Their natural range is across the lowlands of northeastern Mexico. Feral birds have bred in urban communities of southern California, southern Florida, and the island of Oahu in Hawaii. Birds in the Rio Grande Valley of Texas may be either feral, descendants of natural vagrants from Mexico, or both.

Behaviour

They gather in large flocks being noisiest in the morning and evening. The characteristic screeching heard of these birds usually occurs when they travel in a large flock to a new feeding area. Diet consists of seeds, fruits, flowers and nectar. Red-crowned Amazons nest in tree cavities like most other parrots.

Aviculture

This parrot is often kept as a pet and can be very affectionate and playful when given the attention they need from their owners. Although some are excellent talkers, they are best at mimicking sounds and even copy voices.
Source (edited): "http://en.wikipedia.org/wiki/Red-crowned_Amazon"

Red-eared slider

The **red-eared slider** (*Trachemys scripta elegans*) is a semiaquatic turtle belonging to the family Emydidae. It is a subspecies of pond slider. It is the most popular pet turtle in the United States and also popular in the rest of the world. It is native only to the southern United States, but has become established in other places because of pet releases.

Name

Red-eared sliders are popular pets around the world.

Red-eared sliders get their name from the distinctive red mark around their ears. The "slider" part of their name comes from their ability to slide off rocks and logs and into the water quickly. This species was previously known as Troost's turtle in honor of an American herpetologist; *Trachemys scripta troostii* is now the scientific name for another subspecies, the Cumberland slider.

Behavior

Red-eared slider basking on a floating platform under a sunlamp

Red-eared sliders are almost entirely aquatic, but leave the water to bask in the sun and lay eggs. These reptiles are deceptively fast and are also decent swimmers. They hunt for prey and will attempt to capture it when the opportunity presents itself. They are aware of predators and people, and generally shy away from them. The red-eared slider is known to frantically slide off rocks and logs when approached.

Contrary to the popular misconception, red-eared sliders do not have saliva. They, like most aquatic turtles, have fixed tongues, so they must eat their food in water.

Description

The female red-eared slider grows to be 25–33 cm (10–13 in) in length and males 20–25 cm (8–10 in). The red stripe on each side of the head distinguishes the red-eared slider from all other North American species. The carapace (top shell) is oval and flattened (especially in the male), has a weak keel that is more pronounced in the young, and the rear marginal scutes are notched. The carapace usually consists of a dark green background with light and dark highly variable markings. The plastron (bottom shell) is yellow with dark, paired, irregular markings in the center of most scutes. The plastron is highly variable in pattern. The head, legs, and tail are green with fine, yellow, irregular lines. Some dimorphism occurs between males and females. Male turtles are usually smaller than females but their tail is much longer and thicker. Claws are elongated in males which facilitate courtship and mating. Typically, the cloacal opening of the female is at or under the rear edge of the carapace, while the male's opening occurs beyond the edge of the carapace. Older males can sometimes have a melanistic coloration, being a dark grayish-olive green, with markings being very subdued. The red stripe on the sides of the head may be difficult to see or be absent.

Diet

Red-eared sliders are omnivores and eat a variety of animal and plant materials in the wild including, but not limited to, fish, crayfish, carrion, tadpoles, snails, crickets, wax worms, aquatic insects and numerous aquatic plant species. The captive diet for pet red-eared sliders should be a varied diet consisting of invertebrates such as worms, aquatic and land plants, and other natural foods. They should never be fed commercial dog food or cat food. Calcium (for shell health) can be supplemented by adding pieces of cuttlebone to the diet, or with commercially available vitamin and mineral supplements. A nutritious food readily accepted by young turtles is baby clams soaked in krill oil covered with powdered coral calcium. Younger turtles tend to be more carnivorous (eat more animal protein) than adults. As they grow larger and older, they become increasingly herbivorous. Live foods are particularly enjoyed and add to the quality of life of captive turtles. Providing a wide variety of foods is the key to success with captive red-eared sliders. For pet red eared slider turtles, one can feed them treats occasionlly, like shrimp, chicken, cucumbers, or tomatoes. Larger turtles have been known to prey upon younger turtles.

Hibernation

Reptiles do not hibernate, but actually brumate, becoming less active, but occasionally rising for food or water. Brumation can occur in varying degrees. Red-eared sliders brumate over the winter at the bottom of ponds or shallow lakes; they become inactive, generally, in October, when temperatures fall below 10 °C (50 °F). Individuals usually brumate under water. They have also been found under banks and hollow stumps and rocks. In warmer winter climates, they can become active and come to the surface for basking. When the temperature begins to drop again, however, they will quickly return to a brumation state. Sliders will generally come up for food in early March to as late as the end of April. Red-eared sliders kept captive indoors should not brumate. To prevent attempted brumation in an aquarium, lights should be on for 12–14 hours per day and the water temperature should be maintained between 24 and 27 °C (75 and 81 °F). Water temperatures must be under 13 °C (55 °F) for aquatic turtles to brumate properly. Controlling temperature changes to simulate natural seasonal fluctuations encourages mating behavior.

Reproduction

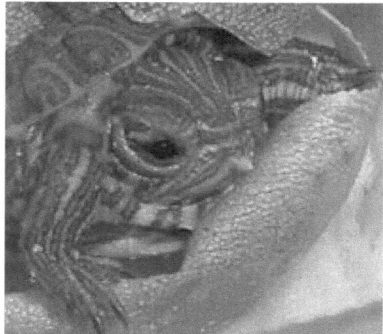

Hatching turtle with its egg-tooth.

Female laying eggs in a nest she dug out with her hind legs

Courtship and mating activities for red-eared sliders usually occur between March and July, and take place under water. The male swims toward the female and flutters or vibrates the back side of his long claws on and around her face and head. The female swims toward the male and, if she is receptive, sinks to the bottom for mating. If the female is not receptive, she may become aggressive towards the male. The courtship can take up to 45 minutes, but the mating itself usually takes only 10 to 15 minutes.

Sometimes a male will appear to be courting another male. This is actually a sign of dominance, and they may begin to fight. Juveniles may display the courtship dance, but until the turtles are five years of age, they are not mature and are unable to mate.

After mating, the female spends extra time basking to keep her eggs warm. She may also have a change of diet, eating only certain foods or not eating as much as she normally would. Mating begins in May and egg-laying occurs in May through early July. A female might lay from two to 30 eggs, with larger females having larger clutches. One female can lay up to five clutches in the same year, and clutches are usually spaced twelve to thirty-six days apart. The time between mating and egg laying can be days or weeks.

Hatching

Eggs hatch 60 to 90 days after they have been laid. Late season hatchlings may spend the winter in the nest and emerge when the weather warms in the spring. Just prior to hatching, the egg contains 50% turtle and 50% egg sac.

A new hatchling breaks open its eggs with its egg-tooth, which falls out about an hour after hatching. This egg tooth never grows back. Hatchlings may stay inside their eggshells after hatching for the first day or two. When a hatchling decides to leave the shell, it has a small sac protruding from its plastron. The yolk sac is vital and provides nourishment while visible and several days after it has been absorbed into the turtle's belly.

Damage or motion enough to allow air into the turtle's body results in death. This is the main reason for marking the top of turtle eggs if their relocation for any reason is required. An egg that has been turned upside down will eventually terminate the embryo growth by the sac smothering the embryo. If it manages to reach term, the turtle will try to flip over with the yolk sac, which allows air into the body cavity and death follows. The other fatal danger is water getting into the body cavity before the sac is absorbed completely and the opening has not completely healed yet. It takes 21 days between the egg opening until water entry.

The sac must be absorbed, and does not fall out. The split may be noticeable in the hatchling's plastron on turtles found in the field, indicating the age of the turtle to be about three weeks old. The split must heal on its own before allowing the turtle to swim. However, this does not mean there is no need for moisture throughout the first three weeks of life outside of the egg. A good idea is to place the hatchlings on moist paper towels. The eggs should be kept on the moist towels from the day they are laid (dig them up an hour after being laid) and covered with toweling until they hatch and can swim. The turtle can also suck the water it needs from the toweling. Red-ear slider eggs matriculate in South Florida in 91 days while in New York City the egg takes 102 days. Turtles which were relocated exhibited this effect with constancy.{{Citation needed|date=April 2008)

As pets

Trachemys scripta elegans

The red-eared slider, often sold cheaply, is the most common type of water turtle kept as pets. As with other turtles, tortoises and box turtles, individuals that survive their first year or two can be expected to live almost as long as their owners. Individuals of this species have lived at least 35 years in captivity.

Red-eared sliders can be quite aggressive—especially when food is involved. If being kept as a pet, care must be taken to prevent injury or even death of its smaller tankmates. However, the opposite can occur if shrimp are introduced as food. Smaller red-eared sliders less than a year old have been known to choke on the shells of the shrimp and suffer from lung puncture.

United States federal regulations on commercial distribution

A 1975 U.S. Food and Drug Administration (FDA) regulation bans the sale (for general commercial and public use) of turtle eggs and turtles with a carapace length of less than 4 inches (100 mm). This regulation comes under the Public Health Service Act, and is enforced by the FDA in cooperation with state and local health jurisdictions. The ban was enacted because of the public health impact of turtle-associated *Salmonella*. Turtles and turtle eggs found to be offered for sale in violation of this provision are subject to destruction in accordance with FDA procedures. A fine of up to $1,000 and/or imprisonment for up to one year is the penalty for those who refuse to comply with a valid final demand for destruction of such turtles or their eggs.

Many stores and flea markets still sell small turtles due to an exception in the FDA regulation which allows turtles under 4 inches (100 mm) to be sold "for bona fide scientific, educational, or exhibitional purposes, other than use as pets."

As with many other animals and inanimate objects, the risk of *Salmonella* exposure can be reduced by following basic rules of cleanliness. Small children must be taught to wash their hands immediately after they finish "playing" with the turtle, feeding it, or changing the water.

U.S. state law

Some states have other laws and regulations regarding possession of red-eared slider because they can be an invasive species where they are not native and have been introduced through the pet trade. As of July 1, 2007, it is illegal in Florida to sell any wild type red-eared slider, as they interbreed with the local yellow-bellied slider population – *Trachemys scripta scripta* is another subspecies of pond sliders, and intergrades typically combine the markings of the two subspecies. However, unusual color varieties such as albino and pastel red-eared sliders, which are derived from captive breeding, are still allowed for sale.

Ideal conditions in captivity

- High water quality - Even with powerful filters, frequent water changes are needed. The water should be heated and maintained at approximately 78-82°F(~26-28°C). Room temperature water is not sufficient and can lead to disfigurement and respiratory ailments.
- Ultraviolet B lighting is required for indoor turtles. While an ideal habitat provides real, unfiltered sunlight, UVB lighting is a necessity in habitats without. Glass or plastic between the bulb and the basking area will prohibit natural and artificial UVB light from entering the habitat. The bulb should be placed above the turtle's basking area.
- Hibernation or brumation is not possible indoors at room temperature. Twelve hours of light per day helps prevent brumation.
- Mature female turtles not kept with males can lay infertile eggs. Females can also remain fertile for several years after a mating and lay fertile eggs. Mature females must have a desirable land area in which to lay eggs. Laying eggs in water is not healthy.
- Dystocia (egg binding), the inability to lay eggs due to tank confinement with insufficient or undesirable land areas, shell deformities or nutritional imbalances, is potentially fatal.
- Groups of turtles should have sex ratios of at least two females per male to avoid mating pressure, stress and injuries from overmating.
- Red-eared sliders in captivity (indoor) should be kept in large terrariums. A 10-20 gallon (40-80 liter) tank is sufficient for hatchling red-eared sliders, although they will quickly outgrow them. Much larger tanks are required for adult turtles. A commonly-used guideline is 10 gallons (40 l) of water per 1 inch (2.5 cm) of shell (example: a turtle of 5 inches (13 cm) and a turtle of 8 inches (20 cm) together need 130 gallons (500 l) of space).
- Red-eared sliders should not be kept in a tank with gravel or decorations that the turtle can fit in its mouth, as this can lead to bowel impaction and death. Commonly and cheaply available 20-grit sand (pool filter sand) makes an ideal substrate.
- Basking platforms or stabilized stacks of rocks should be provided so red-eared sliders can climb out of the water and dry off completely. The ideal basking surface temperature is 85-95°F.

Environment

A line of basking red-eared sliders faces an inquisitive mallard.

A male red-eared slider in an outdoor pond with goldfish and koi

Red-eared sliders enjoy large areas where they are free to swim. These turtles also require a basking area, where they can completely leave the water and enjoy the light provided for them. UVB heat lamps are usually the best option and most common among those taking proper care of their turtles. However, UVB heat lamps have not been proven to have the same quality as direct, unfiltered UV rays from the sun. Turtles are recommended to be given time outdoors on days with more sun, even if this is only possible in the spring and summer.

For the basking area, the best choice is a dirt or sand area, if at all possible.

Since these turtles like to climb, flat rocks also make good basking areas, as well as provide areas for entertainment.

Plant life, either fake or real, also increases red-eared slider quality of life, mimicking their natural environment. The real plants can also serve as a source of food.

Turtles enjoy fresh, clean and clear water. A good filter can help accomplish this. Also, once every two weeks, about 25% of the water should be removed and replaced with new water, and the filter cleaned. It is also strongly recommended to keep fast freshwater fish if the tank is large enough and the water has the proper pH and temperature. In a large enough tank with areas for fish to hide, it is very unlikely they will be eaten. Meanwhile, the majority of freshwater fish will feed on the leftover turtle feed, which allows for a much cleaner environment for both the turtles and the fish. They do not fare well in confined quarters, especially when overcrowded with hatchlings. They have been known to be cannibalistic. Certain species of fresh-water fish are also useful in consuming mosquito larvae, which may appear in outdoor enclosures.

Neurophysiology

Extensive research into the workings of the red eared sliders' brains has been performed at Saint Louis University by Prof. Michael Ariel.

In popular culture

Within the second volume of the *Tales of the Teenage Mutant Ninja Turtles* comic the four Turtles are revealed as specimens of the red-eared slider. The popularity of the Turtles led to a craze for keeping them as pets in Great Britain.

It was speculated that people often disposed of unwanted turtles by releasing them into the toilet, including in areas where they do not occur naturally, risking upsetting the originally balanced ecosystem of those particular areas. As a result, red-eared sliders have been considered one of the top 100 invasive species today

Source (edited): "http://en.wikipedia.org/wiki/Red-eared_slider"

Red-masked Parakeet

Juvenile starting to get a few red feathers on its head.

The **Red-masked Parakeet**, *Aratinga erythrogenys*, is a medium-sized parrot from Ecuador and Peru. It is popular as a pet and considered a good talker. It is known in aviculture as the **Cherry-headed Conure**.

Description

Red-masked Parakeets average about 33 cm (13 in) long, of which half is the tail. They are bright green with a mostly red head on which the elongated pale eye-ring is conspicuous; the nape is green. Also, the lesser and median underwing coverts are red, and there is some red on the neck, the thighs, and the leading edge of the wings. Juveniles have green plumage, until their first red feathers appear at around the age of four months.

Its call is two-syllabled, harsh and loud.

Breeding

Clutches average 3 to 4 eggs and incubation is 23 or 24 days. Nests are usually made in tree cavities. Juvenile birds fledge after 50 days with green plumage.

Range

These birds are native to southwestern Ecuador and northwestern Peru, where they inhabit forest edges and partially cleared areas.

Status

It has been the tenth most common Neotropical parrot imported into the USA with over 26,000 parakeets checked in from 1981 to 1985. This bird was formerly more common in its limited range, and only fairly recently has been reclassified from a species of least concern to a species near threatened (1994).

Feral populations

Parrots on Telegraph Hill, San Francisco.

Feral parrots on a street lamp in San Francisco; one has its wings open showing red and green on the underside of a wing

Escaped cage birds are considered to be introduced in Spain. They are also found in Florida, Hawaii, and California, and make up most of the feral population in San Francisco that are documented in the film *The Wild Parrots of Telegraph Hill* by Judy Irving based on the book of the same name by Mark Bittner. Although these birds reproduce in the wild, the Red-masked Parakeet is not considered established in North America. Breeding populations of feral parakeets have been observed in San Diego County, Los Angeles, San Gabriel Valley, Sunnyvale and San Francisco. The birds have been observed feeding on the fruits of the cultivated tropical vegetation and nesting in the ubiquitous palm trees.

Source (edited): "http://en.wikipedia.org/wiki/Red-masked_Parakeet"

Rose-ringed Parakeet

Male at Hodal, Haryana, India.

Female at Hodal, Haryana

The **Rose-ringed Parakeet** (*Psittacula krameri*), also known as the **Ring-necked Parakeet**, is a gregarious tropical parakeet species that has an extremely large range. Since the trend of the population appears to be increasing, the species has been evaluated as Least Concern by IUCN in 2009.

Rose-ringed parakeets are popular as pets. Its scientific name commemorates the Austrian naturalist Wilhelm Heinrich Kramer.

This non-migrating species is one of few parrot species that have successfully adapted to living in 'disturbed habitats', and in that way withstood the onslaught of urbanisation and deforestation. In the wild, this is a noisy species with an unmistakable squawking call.

Description

Rose-ringed parakeets measure on average 40 cm (16 in) in length including the tail feathers. Their average single wing length is about 15–17.5 cm (5.9–6.9 in). The tail accounts for a large portion of their total length.

The Rose-ringed parakeet is sexually dimorphic. The adult male sports a red neck-ring and the hen and immature birds of both sexes either show no neck rings, or display shadow-like pale to dark grey neck rings

Phylogeny and distribution

Four subspecies are recognized, though they do not differ much:
* African subspecies:

African-ringnecked (aka ARN) Parakeet (*P. krameri krameri*): West Africa in Guinea, Senegal and southern Mauritania, east to Western Uganda and Southern Sudan.

Abyssinian-ringnecked (aka Aby-RN) Parakeet (*P. krameri parvirostris*): Northwest Somalia, west across northern Ethiopia to Sennar district, Sudan.
* Asian subspecies:

Indian-ringnecked (aka IRN) Parakeet (*P. krameri manillensis*) originates from the southern Indian subcontinent and has feral and/or naturalized populations worldwide. In Australia, Great Britain (mainly around London), the United States, and other western countries, it is often referred to as the **Indian Ring-Necked Parakeet/Parrot**.

Boreal or Neumann's ringnecked (aka BRN) Parakeet (*P. krameri borealis*) is distributed in Bangladesh, Pakistan, northern India and Nepal to central Burma; introduced populations worldwide in localities.

A phylogenetic analysis using DNA (see *Psittacula*) showed that the Mauritius Parakeet (*Psittacula echo*) is closely related to this species, and probably needs to be placed between the African and Asian subspecies. Consequently, this species is paraphyletic.

Cultural

Represents the bird of Islamabad Capital Territory (unofficial).

Diet

In the wild, Rose-ringed parakeets usually feed on buds, fruits, vegetables, nuts, berries and seeds. Wild flocks also fly several miles to forage in farmlands and orchards causing extensive damage. They have been found to feed extensively on pigeon pea (*Cajanus cajan*) during winter in India. They also breed during winter unlike most other South Asian birds.

Aviculture

Rose-ringed Parakeets are popular as pets and they have a long history in aviculture. The ancient Greeks kept the Indian subspecies *P. krameri manillensis*, and the ancient Romans kept the African subspecies *P. krameri krameri*. Colour mutations of the Indian-ringnecked Parakeet subspecies have become widely available in recent years.

Mimicry

Both males and females have the ability to mimic human speech. First it listens to its surroundings, and then it copies the voice of the human speaker. Some people hand-raise Rose-ringed parakeet chicks for this purpose. Such parrots then become quite tame and receptive to learning. They can also show emotions similar to human beings and adjust easily to family life. They take time to mimic.

Examples of Indian-ringnecked Parakeet colour mutations in aviculture

Blue mutation

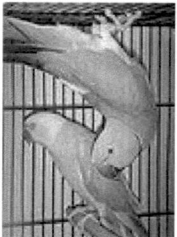
Female is a Parblue Grey and the male is a Parblue Pallid (uncommon mutations).

Female is Lutino, male is Cinnamon Parblue (both juveniles).

Albino male

Feral birds

A feral female in a garden in Bromley, London

The Rose-ringed Parakeet has established feral populations in India, a number of European cities, South Africa and Japan. There are also apparently stable populations in the USA (Florida, California and Hawaii) and a small self-sustaining population in Tunis, Tunisia, and Tehran, Iran (concentrated in the north side of the city). They are also found throughout Lebanon, Israel, UAE, Bahrain, Qatar, and Oman. There are a small number of escaped birds in Australia.

The European populations became established during the mid to late 20th Century from introduced and escaped birds. There are two main population centres in Britain: the largest is based around south London, where they can be regularly seen in places such as Battersea Park, Richmond Park, and Hampstead Heath; the smaller population can be seen in Esher and Berkshire, and by 2005 consisted of many thousands of birds, known as the Kingston parakeets. The winter of 2006 saw three separate roosts of circa 6000 birds around London A smaller population occurs around Margate, Broadstairs and Ramsgate, Kent. Elsewhere in Britain, smaller feral populations have become established from time to time (e.g., at Studland, Dorset, Kensington Gardens, and South Manchester). It has been suggested that feral parrots could endanger populations of native British birds, and that the Rose-ringed Parakeet could even be culled as a result. A major agricultural pest in locations such as India, as of 2011 the Rose-ringed Parakeet population is growing rapidly but is generally limited to urban areas in southern England where their preferred diet of seed, nut, fruits, and berries are available in suburban gardens and bird feeders.

Feral male in Amsterdam, Netherlands

In the Netherlands, the feral population in the four largest urban areas (Amsterdam, Rotterdam, Utrecht and especially in The Hague) has been estimated at more than 10,000 birds, more than double the number of birds estimated in 2004. There also exists a feral population in Belgium, with as many as 5,000 pairs estimated in Brussels. These originate from an original population that was set free in 1987 when the Meli Zoo and Attraction Park near the Atomium was closed to make way for the Brupark. In Germany, these birds are found along the Rhine in all major urban areas like Cologne, Bonn and Heidelberg, Wiesbaden and in the northeast of Hamburg. Other populations are found around Paris, Rome - notably in the gardens of the Palatine Hill and at Villa Borghese, and in Barcelona.

The specimens in these naturalized populations often represent intra-specific hybrids, originally between varying numbers — according to locality — of the subspecies *manillensis*, *borealis*, and/or (to a lesser extent) *krameri* along with some inter-specific hybrids with naturalized *Psittacula eupatria*

(Alexandrine Parakeet).

However, in some parts of South Asia—from where the Rose-ringed Parakeets originated—populations of these birds are decreasing due to trapping for the pet trade. Despite some people's attempts to revive their population by freeing these birds from local markets, the Rose-ringed Parakeet's population has dropped drastically in many areas of the Indian subcontinent.
Source (edited): "http://en.wikipedia.org/wiki/Rose-ringed_Parakeet"

Santa Cruz sheep

Santa Cruz sheep at the Roger Williams Park Zoo

Santa Cruz sheep are an extremely rare breed of domestic sheep that once existed as a feral population on the Santa Cruz Island of the Channel Islands of California. Small and hardy, the sheep were all killed or removed from the island to prevent destruction of natural habitats. Today, they number fewer than 200 animals. This breed is primarily raised for wool.

History

In the mid-19th century, sheep that were most likely of the Merino, Rambouillet (French Merino), or Churro breed were brought to Santa Cruz Island. By the 1860s thousands of sheep grazed freely on the island. Throughout the 20th century, ranching declined on the island and most of the sheep became feral. In 1978, The Nature Conservancy gained control of the island; sheep numbers around this time were estimated to be over 20,000. Later, the Nature Conservancy and the National Park Service began to kill or remove all sheep remaining in order to prevent overgrazing of the island's vegetation. Today, the breed has fewer than 200 animals remaining, and is considered "critical" by the American Livestock Breeds Conservancy. A small population of the sheep exists on the mainland, and were largely placed through adoption.

Characteristics

Like many breeds of island sheep, Santa Cruz sheep are relatively small and extremely hardy: they are good foragers and need no assistance with lambing. However, because of the fine-wooled breeds that they are derived from, Santa Cruz sheep are unique among formerly feral island breeds in their medium to fine wool with a soft feel. Their fleeces are mostly white, but some colored sheep are known among the breed.
Source (edited): "http://en.wikipedia.org/wiki/Santa_Cruz_sheep"

Sato (dog)

a 'sato' or 'Puerto Rican Found Dog'

Sato is a Puerto Rican slang term referring to the feral dogs that inhabit its major cities. They are also known as 'Puerto Rican Found Dogs' in the United States. In Puerto Rico's metropolitan areas, satos can be found living in alleyways, under cars, and between refuse cans. Because of satos' out-of-control numbers and people's view of them as a public menace and health hazard, they are often the victims of abuse such as burning and drowning.

While satos do come in a variety of shapes and sizes, there is some uniformity in their appearance and demeanor. They tend to be small to medium sized, with the largest ones weighing about fifty pounds. Their ears are either pointy, as a terrier's are, or similar to a beagle's. They have pronounced snouts and thick, short-haired coats. Satos are highly intelligent, healthy, and loyal, making them excellent nanny or [companion dogs]. Their features result from years of unchecked breeding amongst a variety of mixed breeds, but there is a distinct lack of qualities found among toy breeds. Most satos are the result of breeding from working and hunting dogs. Most satos live to be 10-12 years old, though many live up to 15 years.

The organization *Save a Sato Foundation* is dedicated to rescuing abused and abandoned satos and finding homes for them. Because of this organization's efforts in placing the dogs and raising awareness about them, satos are becoming more and more popular pets in the United States and have been adopted as far away as Southern France. In December 1999, the foundation arranged for four sato puppies to be sent from Puerto Rico to a humane society in Orlando, Florida which would arrange for them to be adopted.

Also see
- Free-ranging urban dog
- Mixed-breed dog

Source (edited): "http://en.wikipedia.org/wiki/Sato_(dog)"

Semi-feral

A **semi-feral** animal is an animal that lives predominantly in a feral state, but has some contact and experience with humans. This may be due to having been born into a domesticated state and then reverting to life in wild conditions, or it may be an animal that grows up in essentially wild conditions but has developed a comfort level with humans due to feeding, receiving medical care, or similar contacts.

Definitions of *semi-feral* in relation to cats vary, but essentially describe an originally domesticated cat that has reverted to the wild and is no longer owned or kept by someone. Semi-feral cats may continue to live in proximity to humans and may be accustomed to their presence. Feral cats on the other hand are generally agreed to be the descendants of domesticated cats that have themselves never been domesticated. A semi-feral cat that mates and gives birth to a litter will produce feral offspring.

In the context of horses and horse breeds, semi-feral animals are those which are often untrained but usually owned by individuals. They are allowed to run in a natural state approaching that of wild conditions, but are periodically rounded up for assorted reasons, such as to wean foals, administer routine or emergency veterinary care, and so on. An example is the Camargue horse of France. Truly feral horses, such as the American Mustang or Australian Brumby have domesticated ancestors, but generally have no human ownership and live in essentially wild conditions, though they may also occasionally be rounded up for various management purposes. A true wild horse can only be a horse without any domesticated ancestors. The only living, truly wild horse is the Przewalski's horse.

Source (edited): "http://en.wikipedia.org/wiki/Semi-feral"

Stray dogs in Bangkok

It is estimated that there are over 120,000 stray dogs in Bangkok, Thailand. The management of these so-called *soi* dogs has become a serious problem in the capital.

Status

Most of the 300,000 stray dogs in Bangkok are not aggressive, and many have been injured in traffic. However, strays occasionally attack people, and few have been vaccinated against canine diseases.

Management

In the 1990s, more than 200 dogs were euthanized each day. In 1998, however, the Society for the Prevention of Cruelty to Animals campaigned against the practice, which they argued violated Buddhist principles. The campaign generated substantial public outcry against the euthanization of dogs, and the city adopted a pro-life dog policy.

A recent regulation has forbidden the feeding of stray dogs in public places.

In September 2007, the Bangkok Metropolitan Administration began a program of mandatory registration for dogs; the program was aimed to deter the abandonment of dogs, which could be traced to their owners. Requirements for such registration include the implantation of a microchip identifying the owner, rabies vaccination for dogs less than one year old, and sterilization; dog owners were required to register their pets before July 2008. Starting on July 4, 2008, dogs found unregistered may be sent to a dog kennel in the northern province of Uthai Thani and their owners may be fined up to 5,000 baht. Critics of mandatory registration have asserted that it has actually increased the number of strays, as dog owners who do not wish to pay for implementation are abandoning their pets rather than risking receiving fines.

Before prominent events, stray dogs have been rounded up and sent to shelters. This occurred before the 2003 Asia-Pacific Economic Cooperation, when thousands of dogs were removed from the city and sent to the Livestock Development Department's animal quarantine stations in Phetchaburi and Sa Kaeo provinces. Stray dogs were again transported from the city in preparation for the king's 2006 anniversary celebration, with efforts focusing on areas near expensive hotels where royal guests stayed. These strays were sent to the kennel in Uthai Thani, where it was planned they would stay until their death.

In culture

The 2006 Thai movie *Kao Niew Moo Ping* by Siwaporn Pongsuwan focused on the relationship between a runaway girl and the stray dog she befriends.

Source (edited): "http://en.wikipedia.org/wiki/Stray_dogs_in_Bangkok"

Sulphur-crested Cockatoo

The **Sulphur-crested Cockatoo**, *Cacatua galerita*, is a relatively large white cockatoo found in wooded habitats in Australia and New Guinea. They can be locally very numerous, leading to them sometimes being considered pests. They are well known in aviculture, although they can be demanding pets.

Distribution

In Australia, Sulphur-crested Cockatoos can be found widely in the north and east, ranging as far south as Tasmania, but avoiding arid inland areas with few trees. They are numerous in suburban habitats in cities such as Adelaide, Canberra, Sydney and Brisbane. Except for highland areas, they occur throughout most of New Guinea and on nearby smaller islands such as Waigeo, Misool and Aru, and various islands in the Cenderawasih Bay and Milne Bay.

There are four recognised subspecies; *C. g. triton* (Temminck, 1849) is found in New Guinea and the surrounding islands, *C. g. elenora* (Finsch, 1867) is restricted to the Aru Islands between Australia and New Guinea, *C. g. fitzroyi* (Mathews, 1912) in northern Australia from West Australia to the Gulf of Carpentaria and the nominate subspecies which is found from Cape York to Tasmania.

Introduced species

Within Australia, Sulphur-crested Cockatoos of the nominate race have also been introduced to Perth, which is far outside the natural range. Outside Australia, they have been introduced to Singapore, where their numbers have been estimated to be between 500 and 2000. They have also been introduced to Palau and New Zealand. In New Zealand the introduced populations may number less than 1000. This species has also been recorded from various islands in Wallacea (e.g. Kai Islands and Ambon), but it is unclear if it has managed to become established there.

Description

In Brisbane, Queensland.

It has a total length of 45–55 cm (18–22 in), with the Australian subspecies larger than subspecies from New Guinea and nearby islands. The plumage is overall white, while the underwing and tail are tinged yellow. The expressive crest is yellow. The bill is black, the legs are grey, and the eye-ring is whitish. Males typically have almost black eyes, whereas the females have a more red or brown eye, but this require optimum viewing conditions to be seen. The differences between the subspecies are subtle. *C. g fitzroyi* is similar to the nominate race but lacks the yellow on the ear tufts and slightly blueish skin around the eye. *C. g. eleonora* is similar to *C. g. fitzroyi* but is smaller and has broader feathers in the crest, and *C. g. triton* is similar to *C. g. eleonora* except it has a smaller bill.

It is similar in appearance to the three species of corellas found in Australia. However, corellas are smaller, lack the prominent yellow crest and have pale bills. In captivity, the Sulphur-crested Cockatoo is easily confused with the smaller Yellow-crested Cockatoo or the Blue-eyed Cockatoo with a differently shaped crest and a darker blue eye-ring.

Behaviour

Walking on grass in Tasmania, Australia

Their distinctive raucous call can be very loud; it is adapted to travel through the forest environments in which they live, including tropical and subtropical rainforests. These birds are naturally curious, as well as very intelligent. They have adapted very well to European settlement in Australia and live in many urban areas.

These birds are very long-lived, and can live upwards of 70 years in captivity, although they only live to about 20–40 years in the wild. They have been known to engage in geophagy, the process of eating clay to detoxify their food. These birds produce a very fine powder to waterproof themselves instead of oil as many other creatures do.

The Sulphur-crested Cockatoo is a seasonal breeder in Australia, little is known about its breeding behaviour in New Guinea. In southern Australia the breeding season is from August to January, whereas in northern Australia the season is from May to September. The nest is a bed of wood chips in a hollow in a tree. Like many other parrots it competes with others of its species and with other species on nesting sites. Two to three eggs are laid and incubation lasts between 25–27 days. Both parents incubate the eggs and raise the nestlings. The nestling period is between 9 to 12 weeks, and the young fledgelings remain with their parents for a number of months after fledging.

A 2009 study involving an Eleonora Cockatoo (the subspecies *Cacatua galerita eleonora*) named Snowball found that Sulphur-crested Cockatoos are capable of synchronising movements to a musical beat.

Pest status

Numerous cockatoos causing damage to a shopping centre facade

In some parts of Australia, the Sulphur-crested Cockatoo can be very numerous, and may cause damage to cereal and fruit crops. They can also be destructive to timber structures such as house planking, garden furniture and trees. Consequently, they are sometimes shot or poisoned as pests. Government permit is required, as they are a protected species under the Australian Commonwealth Law.

Aviculture

Sulphur-crested Cockatoos may no longer be imported into the United States as a result of the Wild Bird Conservation Act. However, they have been bred in captivity. They are demanding pets, being very loud and having a natural desire to chew wood and other hard and organic materials.

Cocky Bennett of Tom Ugly's Point in Sydney was a celebrated Sulphur-crested Cockatoo who reached an age of 100 years or more. He had lost his feathers and was naked for much of his life, and died in the early years of the twentieth century. His body was stuffed and preserved after death. Another 'Cocky', born in 1921 and residing in Arncliffe with his owner Charlie Knighton, was 76 years old in the late 1990s.

Sulphur-crested Cockatoos, along with many other parrots, are susceptible to Psittacine Beak and Feather Disease, a viral disease, which causes birds to lose their feathers and grow grotesquely shaped beaks. The disease occurs naturally in the wild, and in captivity.
Source (edited): "http://en.wikipedia.org/wiki/Sulphur-crested_Cockatoo"

Trap-Neuter-Return

Trap-Neuter-Return (TNR), also known as Trap-Test-Vaccinate-Alter-Release (TTVAR), is a method of humanely trapping unaltered feral cats, neutering them, and releasing them back to the same environment where they were collected. TNR is promoted by proponents as a humane and more effective alternative to animal control for managing and reducing feral cat (and dog) populations. Opponents claim that the procedure has negative impacts on wildlife (especially birds) and contend that the program poses health risks to local communities; they assert that it has failed to demonstrate any consistent measure of success at reducing feral cat populations.

Methodology

Feral cat recovering from spay surgery.

Feral kitten, approximately nine months old, with the tip of his left ear removed to indicate he has been trapped and neutered.

Trap-Neuter-Return begins with the trapping of feral cats using humane cage traps. The captured feral cats are taken (in the trap) to a veterinary clinic where they are sterilized by the castration of males and spaying of females. Typical TNR programs also involve providing the cats vaccinations against certain diseases like rabies, feline panleukopenia, herpes, and calicivirus. Finally the cats are marked so that they can be easily identified as a sterilized feral, usually by cropping the pointed end of the ear so that it has a square appearance (known as *ear tipping*) or cutting a notch at the tip or on the side of the ear.

In some programs the cat might also be tested for feline leukemia virus (FeLV) and/or feline immunodeficiency virus (FIV) prior to sterilization, and possibly euthanized if the test is positive. The value of FIV/FeLV testing is the subject of debate among feral cat advocates, with some stating that doing testing is an ineffective use of limited funds that otherwise could be used to sterilize more cats, and others holding the position that it is unethical (and inhumane) to release a cat that is carrying a virus that causes deadly disease and that is transmissible to other cats.

After the cat is sterilized and vaccinated, it is placed back in the trap and allowed to recover from surgery. It is subsequently released to the site of capture.

Rationale

Practitioners of TNR apparently embrace it as part of a "no-kill" philosophy: that mass killing should never be used as a method of population control. Also, TNR advocates will claim that the traditional methods of trapping-and-removing will not work because of a so-called "vacuum effect": As some cats are taken out of their territory, others will eventually move in to replace them, which renders the initial removal ineffective. If other feral cats are available to do so, the primary factor of whether they will or not is the availability of food: If enough food is present, then any nearby cats may move in.

Studies have been conducted to gauge the effectiveness of TNR. Several of them suggest that the procedure works, but others question that claim.

A PhD study in North Carolina suggested that although high levels of sterilization could theoretically reduce numbers of cats, in practice they do not because of new immigration by more cats Only one peer-reviewed study showed a reduction in numbers of cats with TNR, and only when 50% of cats were removed for an adoption program; thus it is safe to say that TNR simply does not work in itself to control cat numbers A study by Castillo(2003) is further evidence that TNR does not work. and a review article by Longcore et al. (2009) claiming that TNR programs are not effective at reducing populations of feral cats. New Mexico State University researchers published a study indicating that 71–94 % of a population must be sterlized for the population to decline assuming there is no immigration. The authors point to some long-term studies in which populations did not decrease and in several cases increased due to increased dumping of cats. The authors argue that populations are not stable and movement of cats is significant between urban areas and nearby woodland, and that cats reach high densities when there is a reliable food source.

Effect on wildlife

The Trap-Neuter-Return approach is controversial. Feral cats, which are considered an introduced species in all parts of the world, predate upon wildlife. Many wildlife and bird advocacy organizations argue that TNR does nothing to address this issue or the possibility that predation by feral cats could threaten endangered species. TNR groups state that the cats are scapegoats blamed for the effect of habitat destruction caused by irresponsible human development.

Longcore et al. (2009) in their analysis found that feral cats harm wildlife on continents as well as islands and recorded instances of bird extinction from feral cats on islands and harm to wildlife on continents. Longcore et al. argue that fragmented ecosystems near urban areas are similar to islands and more susceptible to feral cat damage, and that feral cats in urban areas also pose significant risk to migratory birds. The authors argue that feral cats are exotic and do not fill an existing niche and that even well-fed cats significantly impact on wildlife. The article details population and comparative studies of the adverse effects of feral and free roaming cats on birds and other wildlife. The authors also argue that feral cats act as vectors for diseases that can impact on domestic cats, wildlife and humans, examples include feline leukemia virus, feline immunodeficiency virus, fleas, ear mites, hookworms, roundworms, *Bartonella*, *Rickettsia*, *Coxiella* and *Toxoplasma gondii*, and that fecal matter from feral and free-roaming cats has also shown to degrade water quality.

Source (edited): "http://en.wikipedia.org/wiki/Trap-Neuter-Return"

Wild boar

Wild boar, also **wild pig**, (*Sus scrofa*) is a species of the pig genus *Sus*, part of the biological family Suidae. The species includes many subspecies. It is the wild ancestor of the domestic pig, an animal with which it freely hybridises. Wild boar are native across much of Northern and Central Europe, the Mediterranean Region (including North Africa's Atlas Mountains) and much of Asia as far south as Indonesia. Populations have also been artificially introduced in some parts of the world, most notably the Americas and Australasia, principally for hunting. Elsewhere, populations have also become established after escapes of wild boar from captivity.

Name

The term *boar* is used to denote an adult male of certain species — including, confusingly, domestic pigs. However, for wild boar, it applies to the whole species, including, for example, "wild boar sow" or "wild boar piglet".

Wild boar are also known by various names, including **wild hogs** or simply **boars**. In North America they are more commonly referred to as **razorbacks** or **European boars**.

Physical characteristics

The skull of a wild boar found at Lan Lo Au, Hoi Ha Wan Marine Park, Hong Kong

Wild boar skeleton

The body of the wild boar is compact; the head is large, the legs relatively short. The fur consists of stiff bristles and usually finer fur. The colour usually varies from dark grey to black or brown, but there are great regional differences in colour; even whitish animals are known from central Asia. During winter the fur is much denser.

Adult boars average 120–180 cm in length and have a shoulder height of 90 cm. As a whole, their average weight is 50–90 kg kilograms (110–200 pounds), though boars show a great deal of weight variation within their geographical ranges. In central Italy their weight usually ranges from 80 to 100 kg; boars shot in Tuscany have been recorded to weigh 150 kg (331 lb). A French specimen shot in Negremont forest in Ardenne in 1999 weighed 227 kg (550 lb). Carpathian boars have been recorded to reach weights of 200 kg (441 lb), while Romanian and Russian boars can reach weights of 300 kg (661 lb). Generally speaking, native Eurasian boars follow Bergmann's rule, with smaller boars nearer the tropics and larger, smaller-eared boars in the North of their range.

Adult males develop tusks, continuously growing teeth that protrude from the mouth, from their upper and lower canine teeth. These serve as weapons and tools. The upper tusks are bent upwards in males, and are regularly ground against the lower ones to produce sharp edges. The tusks normally measure about 6 cm (2.4 in), in exceptional cases even 12 cm (4.7 in). Females also have sharp canines, but they are smaller, and not protruding like the males' tusks.

Wild boar piglets are coloured differently from adults, having ochre, chocolate and cream coloured stripes lengthwise over their bodies. The stripes fade by the time the piglet is about 6 months old, when the animal takes on the adult's grizzled grey or brown colour (see photo in Reproduction section to compare adult and juvenile colouring). Litter size of wild boars may vary depending on their location. A study in the Great Smoky Mountains National Park in the US reported a mean litter size of 3.3. A similar study on Santa Catalina Island, California reported a mean litter size of 5. Larger litter sizes have been reported in the Middle East.

Behaviour/social structure

Young wild boar.

Adult males are usually solitary outside of the breeding season, but females and their offspring (both sub-adult males and females) live in groups called *sounders*. Sounders typically number around 20 animals, although groups of over 50 have been seen, and will consist of 2 to 3 sows; one of which will be the dominant female. Group structure changes with the coming and going of farrowing females, the migration of maturing males (usually when they reach around 20 months) and the arrival of unrelated sexually active males.

Two wild boars in the snow.

Wild boar are situationally crepuscular or nocturnal, foraging in early morning and late afternoon or at night, but resting for periods during both night and day. They are omnivorous scavengers, eating almost anything they come across, including grass, nuts, berries, carrion, roots, tubers, refuse, insects and small reptiles. Wild boar in Australia are also known to be predators of young deer and lambs.

If surprised or cornered, a boar (particularly a sow with her piglets) can and will defend itself and its young with intense vigor. The male lowers its head, charges, and then slashes upward with his tusks. The female, whose tusks are not visible, charges with her head up, mouth wide, and bites. Such attacks are not often fatal to humans, but may result in severe trauma, dismemberment, or blood loss.

Reproduction

Piglets nursing

Sexual activity and testosterone production in males is triggered by decreasing day length, reaching a peak in mid-autumn. The normally solitary males then move into female groups, and rival males fight for dominance, whereupon the largest and most dominant males achieve the most mating.

The age of puberty for sows ranges from 8 to 24 months of age depending on environmental and nutritional factors. Pregnancy lasts approximately 115 days and a sow will leave the group to construct a mound-like nest, 1–3 days before giving birth (farrowing).

The process of giving birth to a litter lasts between 2 and 3 hours, and the sow and piglets remain in, or close to, the nest for 4–6 days. Sows rejoin the group after 4–5 days, and the piglets will cross suckle between other lactating sows.

Litter size is typically 4-6 piglets but may be smaller for first litter, usually 2-3. The sex ratio at birth is 1:1. Piglets weigh 750g - 1000g at birth. Rooting behaviour develops in piglets as early as the first few days of life, and piglets are fully weaned after 3–4 months. They will begin to eat solid foods such as worms and grubs after about 2 weeks.

Range

Reconstructed range

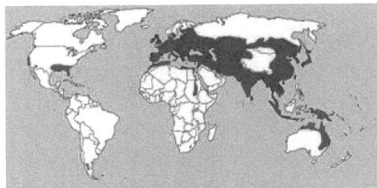

Reconstructed range of wild boar (green) and introduced populations (blue). Not shown are smaller introduced populations in South America, Caribbean, sub-Saharan Africa and elsewhere.

Wild boar were originally found in North Africa and much of Eurasia; from the British Isles to Korea and the Sunda Islands. The northern limit of its range extended from southern Scandinavia to southern Siberia and Japan. Within this range it was absent in extremely dry deserts and alpine zones.

A few centuries ago it was found in North Africa along the Nile valley up to Khartum and north of the Sahara. The reconstructed northern boundary of the range in Asia ran from Lake Ladoga (at 60°N) through the area of Novgorod and Moscow into the southern Ural, where it reached 52°N. From there the boundary passed Ishim and farther east the Irtysh at 56°N. In the eastern Baraba steppe (near Novosibirsk) the boundary turned steep south, encircled the Altai Mountains, and went again eastward including the Tannu-Ola Mountains and Lake Baikal. From here the boundary went slightly north of the Amur River eastward to its lower reaches at the China Sea. At Sachalin there are only fossil reports of wild boar. The southern boundaries in Europe and Asia were almost everywhere identical to the sea shores of these continents. In dry deserts and high mountain ranges, the wild boar is naturally absent. So it is absent in the dry regions of Mongolia from 44–46°N southward, in China westward of Sichuan and in India north of the Himalaya. In high altitudes of Pamir and Tien Shan they are also absent; however, at Tarim basin and on the lower slopes of the Tien Shan they do occur.

Present range

In recent centuries, the range of wild boar has changed dramatically, largely due to hunting by humans and more recently because of captive wild boar escaping into the wild. For many years populations dwindled. They probably became extinct in Great Britain in the 13th century. In Denmark the last boar was shot at the beginning of the 19th century, and in 1900 they were absent in Tunisia and Sudan and large areas of Germany, Austria and Italy. In Russia they were extinct in wide areas in the 1930s.

A revival of boar populations began in the middle of the last century. By 1950 wild boar had once again reached their original northern boundary in many parts of their Asiatic range. By 1960 they reached Saint Petersburg and Moscow, and by 1975 they were to be found in Archangelsk and Astrakhan. In the 1970s they again occurred in Denmark and Sweden, where captive animals escaped and now survive in the wild. (The wild boar population in Sweden was estimated to be around 80,000 in 2006 but is now considered to be in excess of 100,000). In the 1990s boar migrated into Tuscany in Italy. In England, wild boar populations re-established themselves in the 1990s, after escaping from specialist farms that had imported European stock.

Elsewhere, in 1493, Christopher Columbus brought 8 hogs to the West Indies. Importation to the American mainland was in the mid 16th century by Hernan Cortes and Hernando de Soto, and in the mid 17th century by Sieur de La Salle. Pure Eurasian boar were also imported there for sport hunting in the early 20th century. Large populations of wild boar also live in Australia, New Zealand and North and South America.

Status in Britain

Between their medieval extinction and the 1980s, when wild boar farming began, only a handful of captive wild boar, imported from the continent, were present in Britain. Occasional escapes of wild boar from wildlife parks have occurred as early as the 1970s, but since the early 1990s significant populations have re-established themselves after escapes from farms; the number of which has increased as the demand for wild boar meat has grown.

A 1998 MAFF (now DEFRA) study on wild boar living wild in Britain confirmed the presence of two populations of wild boar living in Britain; one in Kent/East Sussex and another in Dorset.

Another DEFRA report, in February 2008, confirmed the existence of these two sites as 'established breeding areas' and identified a third in Gloucestershire/Herefordshire; in the Forest of Dean/Ross on Wye area. A 'new breeding population' was also identified in Devon.

Populations estimates were;
- The largest population, in Kent/East Sussex, was estimated at approximately 200 animals in the core distribution area.
- The second largest, in Gloucestershire/Herefordshire, was estimated to be in excess of 100 animals.
- The smallest, in west Dorset, was estimated to be fewer than 50 animals.
- Since winter 2005/6 significant escapes/releases have also resulted in animals colonising areas around the fringes of Dartmoor, in Devon. These are considered as an additional single 'new breeding population' and currently estimated to be up to 100 animals.

Population estimates for the Forest of Dean are disputed. In early 2010 the Forestry Commission embarked on a cull, with the aim of reducing the boar population from an estimated 150 animals to 100. By August is was stated that efforts were being made to reduce the population from 200 to 90, but that only 25 had been killed. The failure to meet cull targets was confirmed in February 2011.

There have also been reports of wild boar having crossed the River Wye into Monmouthshire, Wales. Many other

Wild boar farming in the UK

Captive wild boar in Britain are kept in private or public wildlife collections and in zoos, but exist predominantly on farms. Because wild boar are included in the Dangerous Wild Animals Act 1976, certain legal requirements have to be met prior to setting up a farm. A licence to keep boar is required from the local council, who will appoint a specialist to inspect the premises and report back to the council. Requirements include secure accommodation and fencing, correct drainage, temperature, lighting, hygiene, ventilation and insurance.

The original U.K. wild boar farm stock was mainly of French origin, but from 1987 onwards, farmers have supplemented the original stock with animals of both west European and east European origin. The east European animals were imported from farm stock in Sweden because Sweden, unlike eastern Europe, has a similar health status for pigs to that of Britain. Currently there is no central register listing all the wild boar farms in the UK; the total number of wild boar farms is unknown.

Status in Germany

Recently, Germany has reported a surge in the wild boar population. According to one study, "German wild boar litters have six to eight piglets on average, other countries usually only about four or five." Boar in Germany are also said to be becoming increasingly 'brazen' and intruding further into cities such as Berlin.

Subspecies

A Common wild boar piglet in the Netherlands

Different subspecies can usually be distinguished by the relative lengths and shapes of their lacrimal bones. *S. scrofa cristatus* and *S. scrofa vittatus* have shorter lacrimal bones than European subspecies. Spanish and French boar specimens have 36 chromosomes, as opposed to wild boar in the rest of Europe which possess 38, the same number as domestic pigs. Boars with 36 chromosomes have successfully mated with animals possessing 38, resulting in fertile offspring with 37 chromosomes.

Four subspecies groups are generally recognized:

Western races (*scrofa* group)
- Common Wild Boar *Sus scrofa scrofa*: The most common and most widespread subspecies, its original distribution ranges from France to European Russia. It has been introduced in Italy, Sweden, Norway, the USA and Canada.
- Iberian Wild Boar *Sus scrofa baeticus*: A small subspecies present in the southwestern Iberian Peninsula. Probably a junior synonym of *S. s. meridionalis*.
- Castillian Wild Boar *Sus scrofa castilianus*: Larger than *S. s. baeticus*, it inhabits northern Spain. Probably a junior synonym of *S. s. scrofa*.
- Sardinian Wild Boar *Sus scrofa meridionalis*: A small, almost maneless subspecies from Corsica, Sardinia and Andalusia. Possibly extinct now in its island range.
- Italian Wild Boar *Sus scrofa majori*: A subspecies smaller than *S. s. scrofa* with a higher and wider skull. It occurs in central and southern Italy. Since the 1950s, it has hybridized extensively with introduced *S. s. scrofa* populations.
- *Sus scrofa attila*: A very large, long-maned, yellowish subspecies from eastern Europe to Kazakhstan, northern Caucasus and Iran.
- Barbary Wild Boar *Sus scrofa algira*: Maghreb in Africa. Closely related to, and sometimes considered a junior synonym of, *S. s. scrofa*, but smaller and with proportionally longer tusks. Now quite rare.
- *Sus scrofa lybica*: A small, pale and almost maneless subspecies from Caucasus to the Nile Delta, Turkey and the Balkans. Possibly extinct now.
- *Sus scrofa sennaarensis*: From Egypt and northern Sudan. Former presence in these countries, where became extinct around 1900, is linked to ancient introductions by man, and *S. s. sennaarensis* is probably a junior synonym of *S. s. scrofa*. "Wild boars" now present in Sudan are derived from domestic pigs.
- *Sus scrofa nigripes*: A light-coloured subspecies with dark legs from Tianshan Mountains, Central Asia.

Indian races (*cristatus* group)

Indian wild boar (*Sus scrofa cristatus*) at Ranthambore National Park

- Indian Wild Boar *Sus scrofa cristatus*: A long-maned subspecies with a coat that is brindled black unlike *S. s. davidi*. More lightly built than European boar. Its head is larger and more pointed than that of the European boar, and its ears smaller and more pointed. The plane of the forehead straight, while it is concave in the European. Occurs from the Himalayas south to central India and east to Indochina (north of the Kra Isthmus).
- *Sus scrofa affinis*: This subspecies is smaller than *S. s. cristatus* and found in southern India and Sri Lanka. Validity questionable.
- *Sus scrofa davidi*: A small, long-maned and light brown subspecies

from eastern Iran to Gujarat; perhaps north to Tajikistan.

Eastern races (*leucomystax* group)

- Manchurian Wild Boar *Sus scrofa ussuricus*: A very large (largest subspecies of the wild boar), almost maneless subspecies with a thick coat that is blackish in the summer and yellowish-grey in the winter. From Manchuria and Korea.
- Japanese Wild Boar *Sus scrofa leucomystax*: A small, almost maneless, yellowish-brown subspecies from Japan (except Hokkaido where the wild boar is not naturally present, and the Ryuku Islands where replaced by *S. s. riukiuanus*).
- Ryuku Wild Boar *Sus scrofa riukiuanus*: A small subspecies from the Ryuku Islands.
- Formosan Wild Boar *Sus scrofa taivanus*: A small blackish subspecies from Taiwan.
- *Sus scrofa moupinensis*: A relatively small and short-maned subspecies from most of China and Vietnam. There are significant variations within this subspecies, and it is possible there actually are several subspecies involved. On the contrary, recent evidence suggests the virtually unknown Heude's pig may be identical to (and consequently a synonym of) wild boars from this region.
- Siberian Wild Boar *Sus scrofa sibiricus*: A relatively small subspecies from Mongolia and Transbaikalia.

Sundaic race (*vittatus* group)

- Banded pig *Sus scrofa vittatus*: A small, short-faced and sparsely furred subspecies with a white band on the muzzle. From Peninsular Malaysia, and in Indonesia from Sumatra and Java east to Komodo. Might be a separate species, and shows some similarities with some other species of wild pigs in southeast Asia.

Domestic pig

The domestic pig is usually regarded as a further subspecies; *Sus scrofa domestica* - although sometimes classified as a separate species; *Sus domestica*.

Feral pigs

Feral pigs in the United States (here Cape Canaveral, Florida)

Domestic pigs can escape and quite readily become feral, and feral populations are problematic in several ways. They cause damage to trees and other vegetation, consume agricultural crops, feed on the eggs of ground-nesting birds and turtles, and can carry disease. Feral pigs often interbreed with wild boar, producing descendants similar in appearance to wild boar; these can then be difficult to distinguish from natural or introduced true wild boar. The characterization of populations as feral pig, escaped domestic pig or wild boar is usually decided by where the animals are encountered and what is known of their history. In New Zealand, for example, feral pigs are known as "Captain Cookers" from their supposed descent from liberations and gifts to Māori by explorer Captain James Cook in the 1770s. New Zealand feral pigs are also frequently known as "tuskers", due to their appearance.

One characteristic by which domestic and feral animals are differentiated is their coats. Feral animals almost always have thick, bristly coats ranging in colour from brown through grey to black. A prominent ridge of hair matching the spine is also common, giving rise to the name *razorback* in the southern United States, where they are common. The tail is usually long and straight. Feral animals tend also to have longer legs than domestic breeds and a longer and narrower head and snout.

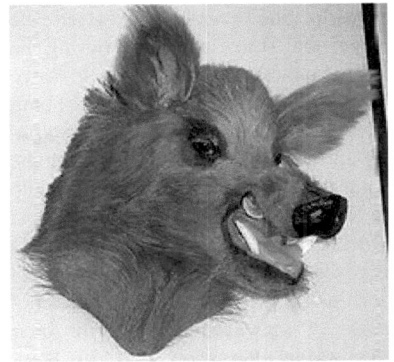

Wild boar/domestic pig hybrid, displayed at Rothschild Museum, Tring, England

A very large swine dubbed Hogzilla was shot in Georgia, United States, in June 2004. Initially thought to be a hoax, the story became something of an internet sensation. *National Geographic Explorer* investigated the story, sending scientists into the field. After exhuming the animal and performing DNA testing, it was determined that Hogzilla was a hybrid of wild boar and domestic swine. As of 2008, the estimated population of 4 million feral pigs caused an estimated US$800 million of property damage a year in the U.S. The problematic nature of feral hogs has caused several states in the U.S. to declare feral hogs to be an invasive species. Often, these states will have greatly-reduced (or even non-existent) hunting regulations regarding feral hogs. In Missouri, no hunting permit is required for the taking of wild boar; hunters may take as many as they like with any weapon. The Missouri Department of Conservation requests that hunters who encounter feral hogs shoot them on sight.

At the beginning of the 20th century, wild boar were introduced for hunting in the United States, where they interbred in parts with free roaming domestic pigs. In South America, New Guinea, New Zealand, Australia and other islands, wild boar have also been introduced by humans and have partially interbred with domestic pigs.

In South America, also during the early 20th century, free-ranging boars were introduced in Uruguay for hunting purposes and eventually crossed the border into Brazil sometime during the 1990s, quickly becoming an invasive species, licensed private hunting of both feral boars and hybrids (*javaporcos*) being allowed from August 2005 on in the Southern Brazilian state of Rio Grande do Sul, although their presence as a pest had been already noticed by the press as early as 1994. Releases and escapes from unlicensed farms (established because of increased demand for boar meat as an alternative to pork), however, continued to bolster feral populations and by mid-2008 licensed hunts had to be expanded to the states of Santa Catarina and São Paulo. Such licensed hunts were, however, forbidden in 2010 by IBAMA, which argued the necessity of additional studies for devising an strategy of pest control for boars. Meanwhile, boars and boar crosses were spotted in the State of Rio de Janeiro, where cases of crop raiding were reported in the municipality of Porciuncula. There's also the danger of an escape from an unlicensed farm in Nova Friburgo. In October 2010, a rural worker was killed by a boar in Ibiá, in the State of Minas Gerais.

Recently established Brazilian boar populations are not to be confused with long established populations of feral domestic pigs (*porcos monteiros*), which have existed mainly in the Pantanal for more than a hundred years, along with native peccaries. The demographic dynamics of the interaction between feral pigs populations and those of the two native species of peccaries (Collared Peccary and White-lipped Peccary) is obscure and is being studied presently. It has been proposed that the existence of feral pigs could somewhat ease jaguar predation on peccary populations, as jaguars would show a preference for hunting pigs, when these are available.

Feral hogs can rapidly increase their population. Sows can have up to 10 offspring per litter, and are able to have two litters per year. Each piglet reaches sexual maturity at 6 months of age. They have virtually no natural predators.

Natural predators

Wild boar are a main food source for tigers in the regions where they coexist. Tigers typically follow boar groups, and pick them off one by one. Tigers have been noted to chase boars for longer distances than with other prey, though they will usually avoid tackling mature male boars. In many cases, boars have gored tigers to death in self defense.

Wolves are also major predators of boars in some areas. Wolves mostly feed on piglets, though adults have been recorded to be taken in Italy, the Iberian Peninsula, and Russia. Wolves rarely attack boars head on, preferring to tear at their perineum, causing loss of coordination and massive blood loss. In some areas of the former Soviet Union, a single wolf pack can consume an average of 50–80 wild boars annually. In areas of Italy where the two animals are sympatric, the extent to which boars are preyed upon by wolves has led to them developing more aggressive behaviour toward both wolves and domestic dogs.

Striped hyenas occasionally feed on boars, though it has been suggested that only hyenas from the three larger subspecies present in Northwest Africa, the Middle East, and India can successfully kill them.

Young piglets are important prey for several species, including large snakes, such as the reticulated python, large birds of prey, and various wild felids. In Australia many piglets are killed by dingos. Adults, due to their size, strength, and defensive aggression, are generally avoided as prey. However, they have been taken additionally by mature leopards; large bears (mainly brown bears); and mature crocodiles. All predators of boars are opportunistic and would take piglets given the opportunity. Where introduced outside of their natural range, boars may be at the top of the food chain, but are also sometimes taken by predators similar to those in their native Eurasia. Introduced wild boars in North America have predators such as the Grizzly bear, Black bear, Gray wolf, Red wolf, coyote, and cougars.

Commercial use

Tyrolean style roasted wild boar

The hair of the boar was often used for the production of the toothbrush until the invention of synthetic materials in the 1930s. The hair for the bristles usually came from the neck area of the boar. While such brushes were popular because the bristles were soft, this was not the best material for oral hygiene as the hairs were slow to dry and usually retained bacteria. Today's toothbrushes are made with plastic bristles.

Boar hair is used in the manufacture of boar-bristle hairbrushes, which are considered to be gentler on hair—and much more expensive—than common plastic-bristle hairbrushes. However, among shaving brushes, which are almost exclusively made with animal fibres, the cheaper models use boar bristles, while badger hair is used in much more expensive models.

Boar hair is used in the manufacture of paintbrushes, especially those used for oil painting. Boar bristle paintbrushes are stiff enough to spread thick paint well, and the naturally split or "flagged" tip of the untrimmed bristle helps hold more paint.

Despite claims that boar bristles have been used in the manufacture of premium dart boards for use with steel-tipped darts, these boards are, in fact, made of other materials and fibres—the finest ones from sisal rope.

In many countries, boar are farmed for their meat, and in countries such as France and Italy, for example, boar (*sanglier* in French, "cinghiale" in Italian) may often be found for sale in butcher shops or offered in restaurants (although the consumption of wild boar meat has been linked to transmission of

Hepatitis E in Japan). In Germany, boar meat ranks among the highest priced types of meat and is as much part of high standard cuisine as venison. In certain countries, such as Laos and parts of China, boar meat is considered an aphrodisiac.

Mythology, religion, history and fiction

Deity form of Varaha, Khajuraho, 12th C AD

The hunt of the Calydonian Boar shown on a Roman frieze (Ashmolean Museum)

The Norse boar Gullinbursti with the god Frey, 1901 painting by Johannes Gehrts

In Celtic mythology the boar was sacred to the Gallic goddess Arduinna, and boar hunting features in several stories of Celtic and Irish mythology. One such story is that of how Fionn mac Cumhaill ("Finn McCool") lured his rival Diarmuid Ua Duibhne to his death—gored by a wild boar

In the *Asterix* comic series set in Gaul, wild boar are the favourite food of Obelix whose immense appetite means that he can eat several roasted boar in a single sitting.

Gullinbursti (meaning "Gold Mane or Golden Bristles") is a boar in Norse mythology.

In Hindu mythology, the third Avatar of the Lord Vishnu was Varaha, a boar.

At least three Roman Legions are known to have had a boar as their emblems: Legio I Italica, Legio X Fretensis and Legio XX Valeria Victrix.

A boar is a long-standing symbol of the city of Milan, Italy. In Andrea Alciato's *Emblemata* (1584), beneath a woodcut of the first raising of Milan's city walls, a boar is seen lifted from the excavation. The foundation of Milan is credited to two Celtic peoples, the Bituriges and the Aedui, having as their emblems a ram and a boar respectively (*Bituricis vervex, Heduis dat sucula signum.*); therefore "The city's symbol is a wool-bearing boar, an animal of double form, here with sharp bristles, there with sleek wool," (*Laniger huic signum sus est, animálque biforme, Aeribus hinc setis, lanitio inde levi*). Alciato credits the most saintly and learned Ambrose for his account.

In Medieval hunting the boar, like the hart, was a 'beast of venery', the most prestigious form of quarry. It was normally hunted by being harboured, or found by a 'limer', or bloodhound handled on a leash, before the pack of hounds were released to pursue it on its hot scent. In The poem *Sir Gawain and the Green Knight* a boar hunt is described, which depicts how dangerous the boar could be to the pack hounds, or raches, which hunted it.

A story from Nevers, which is reproduced in the *Golden Legend*, states that one night Charlemagne dreamed he was about to be killed by a wild boar during a hunt, but was saved by the appearance of a child, who had promised to save the emperor if he would give him clothes to cover his nakedness. The bishop of Nevers interpreted this dream to mean that the child was Saint Cyricus and that he wanted the emperor to repair the roof of the Cathédrale Saint-Cyr-et-Sainte-Julitte de Nevers - which Charlemagne duly did.

The ancient Lowland Scottish Clan Swinton is said to have to have acquired the name Swinton for their bravery and clearing their area of Wild Boar. The chief's coat of arms and the clan crest allude to this legend, as is the name of the village of Swinewood in the county of Berwick which was granted to them in the 11th century.

Richard III (r. 1483–1485) used the white boar as his personal device and badge. It was also passed to his short-lived son, Edward.

Folklore, in the Forest of Dean, England, tells of a giant boar, known as the Beast of Dean, which terrorised villagers in the early 19th century

Coat of Arms of Sauerlach, Germany

Heraldry and other symbolic use

The wild boar and a boar's head are common charges in heraldry. It represents what are often seen as the positive qualities of the boar, namely courage and fierceness in battle. The arms of the Campbell of Possil family (see Carter-Campbell of Possil) include the head, erect and erased of a wild boar, as does the crest Mackinnon clan. The arms of the Swinton Family also possess wild boar, as does the coat of arms of the Purcell family.

Source (edited): "http://en.wikipedia.org/wiki/Wild_boar"

Yellow-crested Cockatoo

The **Yellow-crested Cockatoo**, *Cacatua sulphurea*, also known as the **Lesser Sulphur-crested Cockatoo**, is a medium-sized (approximately 35 cm long) cockatoo with white plumage, bluish-white bare orbital skin, grey feet, a black bill, and a retractile yellow crest. The sexes are similar. *Lessor*, the cockatoo used in the TV series *Baretta*, was a Yellow-crested Cockatoo.

The Yellow-crested Cockatoo is found in wooded and cultivated areas of East Timor and Indonesia's islands of Sulawesi and the Lesser Sundas. It is easily confused with the larger and more common Sulphur-crested Cockatoo, which has a more easterly distribution and can be distinguished by the lack of pale yellow coloring on its cheeks (although some Sulphur-cresteds develop yellowish patches). Also, the Yellow-crested Cockatoo's crest is a brighter color, closer to orange. The Citron-crested Cockatoo, which is a subspecies of the Yellow-crested Cockatoo, is similar, but its crest is orange.

The Yellow-crested Cockatoo's diet consists mainly of seeds, buds, fruits, nuts and herbaceous plants.

Breeding

The Yellow-crested Cockatoo nests in tree cavities. The eggs are white and there are usually two in a clutch. The incubation is shared by both parents. The eggs are incubated for about 28 days and the chicks leave the nest about 75 days after hatching.

Status and conservation

The Yellow-crested Cockatoo is critically endangered. Numbers have declined dramatically due to illegal trapping for the cage-bird trade. Between 1980 and 1992, over 100,000 of these birds were legally exported from Indonesia yet a German proposal submitted to CITES to move it to Appendix I was not approved. It has since been moved to Appendix I. The current population is estimated at as few as 2,500 individuals and is thought to be declining in number.

The subspecies *abbotti* is found only on the island of Masakambing, one of the Masalembu islands. Its population on this tiny island (about 5 km or 1.9 mi) had fallen to 10 as of June and July 2008. The decline results from trapping and logging, especially of mangrove (*Avicennia apiculata*) and kapok trees.

Several national parks provide protection of their habitat, including Rawa Aopa Watumohai National Park on Sulawesi, Komodo National Park in Komodo Island, the national parks of Manupeu Tanah Daru and Laiwangi Wanggameti on Sumba as well as the Nino Konis Santana National Park in East Timor (Timor-Leste).

Introduced population

There is an introduced population of these birds in Hong Kong. They are a common sight across the densely populated area on both sides of the harbour, easily spotted in the woods and public parks in the northern and western of Hong Kong Island. The large group has apparently developed from a number of caged birds that have been released into the Hong Kong skies over many years. An often repeated story is that Hong Kong Governor Sir Mark Aitchison Young released Government House's entire bird collection – including a large number of Yellow-crested Cockatoos – hours before surrendering Hong Kong to Japanese troops in December 1941.

Source (edited): "http://en.wikipedia.org/wiki/Yellow-crested_Cockatoo"